ASSAYS

VOLUME II

ASSAYS

CRITICAL APPROACHES
TO MEDIEVAL AND
RENAISSANCE TEXTS

Peggy A. Knapp
Editor

UNIVERSITY OF PITTSBURGH PRESS

ASSAYS

Critical Approaches to Medieval and Renaissance Texts

is an annual edited by Peggy A. Knapp and published by the University of Pittsburgh Press. The editor is seeking manuscripts which (1) make use of modern critical thought (structuralism, Marxism, psychoanalysis, feminism, and many other kinds) in order to illuminate medieval and Renaissance works (including Milton); (2) argue either for or against the usefulness of one or more contemporary critical stances for clarifying pre-modern works; (3) review the contribution of a particular theory to our understanding of early works; and (4) present the case for older critical methods or outline their relationship to more recent developments. The object is to create an impartial, scholarly forum for debate about the connections between critical theory and early texts.

Please send articles to: The Editor, *Assays*, Department of English, Carnegie-Mellon University, Pittsburgh, Pa. 15213. Manuscripts should be prepared according to the MLA Style Sheet. Send a separate cover letter and return postage together with two copies of each submission. The article itself should not contain or imply the author's name or institutional affiliation, but should begin with the exact title mentioned in the cover letter. The editor is interested in insuring fairness and courtesy to all contributors.

Within the United States, *Assays* may be ordered from the University of Pittsburgh Press, Pittsburgh, Pa. 15260.

Overseas orders should be addressed to Feffer and Simons, Inc., 100 Park Avenue, New York, N.Y. 10017, U.S.A.

Published by the University of Pittsburgh Press, Pittsburgh, Pa. 15260
Copyright © 1983, University of Pittsburgh Press
All rights reserved
Feffer and Simons, Inc., London
Manufactured in the United States of America

Library of Congress Catalog Card Number 80-54059
ISSN 0275-0058
ISBN 0-8229-3468-X

Contents

Editor's Preface

Perhaps even more than at the beginning of this *Assays* adventure, I believe in the importance of being the good neighbor who will help medieval and Renaissance scholarship and contemporary critical theory become more friendly, for, like reason and love in Bottom's view, they keep little company together nowadays. Little, but more all the time. My special concern now is that their proximity doesn't come to produce the mutual suspicion and willful misunderstanding of armed border camps, the one side charging scholarship with closed-mindedness and irrelevancy, the other imputing arrogance and deliberate obfuscation to critical theory, when the truth is that erudition and method are the indispensable components of our professional task.

While volume I ranged widely across the historical and geographical territories in the domain of *Assays*—touching on works from late antiquity to the mid-seventeenth century, from virtually all of Europe—volume II is focused, as it happens, on the fourteenth through sixteenth centuries and on English materials, primarily Chaucer and Shakespeare. The issues raised by postmodernist thought loom larger this time, especially in Robert Knapp's commentary on the implications of retracting and Gary Waller's essay on deconstruction, but in the others too in less obvious ways. Laury Magnus draws some new insights from formalist theory for her reading of the *Franklin's Tale*, Paul Bauschatz enriches our already complex reactions to Chaucer's Pardoner through reference to Augustine and Anselm on lies, Martha Lifson discusses Shakespeare's sonnets in terms of rhetoric and affective stylistics, and Murray Schwartz shows us *Richard II* as both personal and cultural psychic crisis. All these essays, in their different styles, witness an informed and heightened attention to the ways texts speak to and of other texts, address themselves to their audiences, and engage the larger world.

I would like to invite readers to respond to these articulate and controversial discussions, but not in the format, sometimes needlessly acrimonious and trivializing, of letters-to-the-editor. Small matters of correction—additional citiations or objections to phrasing—may be addressed to authors directly. What *Assays* would like to publish are full-scale critical arguments, brief or extended, replying to the ideas, positions, and methods of the essays we have printed. Perhaps in volume III we will be hearing the clash of mighty opposites, pointed, but not fell incenséd.

Assays now has a single editor, as Michael Stugrin has decided to leave academic life. I wish to thank the Advisory Board and expert readers for their good counsel; the University of Pittsburgh Press, especially Catherine Marshall, for intelligent, conscientious, cheerful help with the volume; and Wendy Plesniak, a very able student assistant, for the computer-inputting phase of the work.

ASSAYS

raised in these works. In the more lighthearted tales, such as the
Nun's Priest's, Chaucer uses the philosophical digression simply to
create strata of comic incongruity. But when the reader finds such
ponderous questions infiltrating other narrative contexts which
have more obscure genre warrants, critical commonplaces about
the function of Boethian philosophy can too easily obscure the
more substantial issues: What are such digressions doing here?
Why is such a grandiose question of the problem of evil raised in
the context of an apparently straightforward account of domestic
harmony? What is there about the *Franklin's Tale* that makes
Chaucer decide to forego the economy of narration at which he is
so wonderfully adept? Is the digression absorbed by the narrative,
and if so, how?

These local questions entail broader questions about digression
as a literary device (which, in turn, raise even larger narrative
issues). First, what criteria does a reader, or specifically a Chaucerian reader, use to decide that a certain passage is "digressive"? This
two–part question assumes that the local, Chaucerian answer will
be somewhat different from—though related to—the generic
answer about all digressions. Following Leo Spitzer's line of
thought, one might argue that it is only through the living, moment–to–moment contact with the particulars of a given text,
being fully steeped in the course of its particulars, that the reader
develops a sense of the coherence of the whole through a series of
simultaneous anticipatory and synthetic processes.

This approach would rely heavily on a reader's personal response
to his own intuitions about the shape of a tale. It would, moreover,
imply a certain paradox: artful digressions are false digressions, for
in violating one's intuition of coherence, they underscore the totality of a given structure. In this sense, all literary digressions are
heuristic. Conversely, it is the unartistic, true digression, the digression that *does* wander away from the original point of the
discourse without a meaningful return to the subject, that violates
the real coherence of a narrative. Thus, all artful literary digressions have a specific effect on the subsequent texture of the tale:
some enlargement of the framework or scope of the narration.

Broadening the circumference of the hermeneutic circle, one can
also ask what makes for a Chaucerian digression. Certainly, once
one moves outside the framework of a given tale and toward a
definition of digression in the Chaucerian canon, the problems become more complex. Chaucer's habit of framing his narratives is
crucial here, for though the frame device is fully elastic, allowing a

single narrative construct to "swallow whole" two narratives as widely divergent, say, as the *Parson's Tale* and the *Miller's Tale*, the multiplication of perspectives and/or topoi which the frame engenders can create an unchartable terrain in which digression is barely distinguishable among the text's multiple données.

Yet, strangely enough, the identification of a characteristically Chaucerian digression is also simpler than pinpointing specific digressions, for on this level one can fix on such markers as typical subjects of digression and specific points in the narrative typically chosen as "launching" points. Moreover, it is possible to examine rhetorical modes, tropes, and formulae accompanying—and often directly announcing—a digression. While a detailed description of these features is beyond the scope of this article, a few generalizations about Chaucerian digression can safely be made. First, a great many Chaucerian digressions are both philosophical and allusive in nature, bringing the wisdom of the "clerkes" or other "auctours" to bear on issues of causality. A few noteworthy examples are the narrator's long digression on free will and necessity in the *Nun's Priest's Tale* (3215–52), which invokes the names of "Augustyn," "Boece," and "Bisshop Bradwardyn" in the space of two lines, or in the long meditation on the causes of action in lines 1956–75 and on Fortune in lines 2055–68 in the *Merchant's Tale*. Most of the time, as Bernard L. Jefferson has suggested,[2] the issues or questions raised are left unresolved, and the narrator abruptly takes up the story again, leaving them rankling in the reader's mind as the narration continues.

As this would suggest, Chaucerian digressions are often strongly marked as such. The digression in the *Nun's Priest's Tale* cited above is whimsically preceded by the line "Now wol I torne agayn to my sentence" and is terminated by "I wol nat han to do of swich mateere; / My tale is of a cok, as ye may heere." Sometimes digressions are given to garrulous narrators like Pandarus ("The dayes honour, and the hevenes ye / The nyghtes foo—all this clepe I the sonne—"), or call attention to the needlessness of telling. The *Book of the Duchess*, for example, a tale in which the effect of telling is itself the subject of scrutiny, contains three such tags as "Nay, trewly, I gabbe now" (1075), "But wherefore that y telle my tale?" (1034), and "but thereof no fors." (1170). These self–conscious markers of interruption are so numerous in Chaucer that the reader cannot help being as aware of the act of narration as of the facts of narration.

One might object that relying on such markers begs the question of how the reader recognizes and "processes" a digression, leaving this critical decision in the author's hands. But, as I have argued, Chaucer's digressions indicate his full awareness of the relation of mutual responsiveness. between critic (audience) and writer. A test of the artfulness of the Chaucerian digression is its violence—the extent to which it assaults the audience's angle of vision. And since Chaucer favors the philosophical digression above others, his digressions heighten the audience's awareness of authorial control of the action by raising the question of the relation between philosophical speculation and event. Thus the artifice involved is highly visible in Chaucer, and correlatively, the reintegration of the apparently digressive element must be the more unobrusive and seamless.

In considering this double virtuosity of the Chaucerian digression, another line of modern literary theory is even more relevant than these extrapolations from Spitzer, the line suggested by Russian formalist criticism, and particularly, by Boris Tomashevsky in his seminal essay, "Thematics."[3] Tomashevsky is intrigued by playfully digressive elements in writers such as Cervantes or Sterne who, like Chaucer, take the utmost pleasure in laying bare their own tale–telling chicanery. Tomashevsky's focus on elaborations of form matches, for our purposes, his careful attention to what might be called literary texture—to ways in which certain themes are integrated (or not integrated) with others in the tale. In fact, Tomashevsky attempts to systematize these issues, providing the reader with a quasi–deductive framework for indentifying the digressive and for perceiving its reintegration or nonreintegration with the story. In order to do this, he first distinquishes between "story," the "aggregate of motifs in their logical, causal–chronological order," and "plot," the narrative presentation of causality, or, in other words, the artful manipulation of the elements or motifs of the story.[4]

Those elements of the story which are to be considered nondigressive are called "bound motifs," obligatory in the sense that their omission would destroy the orderly progression of events. On the other hand, those elements "which might be omitted without disturbing the whole causal–chronological course of events are *free motifs.*"[5] In sum, if a motif has no discernible influence on what happens in the tale, it is a free—and in our sense digressive—motif.

Considered carefully, these distinctions imply that a motif may be free for any one of four possible reasons:

(a) Because the writer has negligently introduced it (the case of the careless "trueness" of nonartistic digression).

(b) Because historical or generic canons of artistic coherence may allow or prescribe that certain elements remain free. (Here, an example might be the epic catalogue in which many of the named elements do not recur.)

(c) Because the motif is about to be artistically "bound" to the story's maneuvers. (A quick and obvious Shakespearean example would be the garrulous digressiveness of Polonius—a pointlessness ultimately bound to his own slaughter.) The process implied by this explanation of the free motif is, as I shall argue, of most interest for Chaucer criticism, and is nowhere more evident than in the *Franklin's Tale.*

(d) Because the writer has artfully left the motif free, deliberately refusing to bind this element so as to call attention to the work's own artifice. This is the kind of digression of most interest to the Russian formalists—and Sterne's blank page in *Tristram Shandy* is a perfect example. Of course, this last motivation for digression has its genesis both in more modern texts and in the taste formed by those texts. It would apply to the more open structure, the "self-consuming" kind of artifact. However, I should like to suggest that because of the gap in narrative time before a Chaucerian free motif becomes bound, Chaucer is courting this last motivation—teasing the reader and heightening a desire for coherence.

One cautionary note must be sounded here. Particularly in relation to a medieval text, a (b) account must be considered before either a (c) or a (d), and, even so, there is always the possibility that a (c) account is evidence more of critical inventivness than of authorial design. One final exatrapolation from Tomashevsky's aesthetic is useful as a corrective to such potential misreading.

Tomashevsky distinguishes between the "prop" kind of free motif and a more thematic free motif. A material motif, such as a handkerchief or a character's baldness, is much easier to transmute from a free to a bound motif, for things provide a concrete locus for causual progression, and their use can have obvious consequences. Other, more abstract free motifs, such as pride, "gentillesse," or blindness, can usually be bound only to the plot, that is, to the whole complex narrative system in which internal, character motivation and external, dramatic motivation are finely balanced; though such abstract motifs are often essential to our *understanding* of what happens, they are seldom essential to its happening. Hence, strictly speaking, they remain free motifs. Only in rare instances does an author succeed in binding an abstract free motif to the story as well as to the plot, and it is part of Chaucer's genius that he is able to do so with apparent ease as when, for example, Chauntecleer's pride causes him to "wynke" and thus fall prey to the fox. The conventional maxim that pride goeth before a fall only adds to the inert abstractness of the motif, and it is left to higher craft to dramatize pride's agency.

The even greater triumph of the *Franklin's Tale* is its binding to the story of such disinterested virtues as generosity and "gentillesse," ideals that are ordinarily banished from the realms of agency and action and which, even in the tale itself, initially seem remote from the complications of the narrative. The most puzzling abstraction in its context is, as I have mentioned, Dorigen's challenge of God's wisdom. Her long, digressive questioning is particularly problematic, for it introduces an uncompromisingly free motif. Our "auctour," as usual, is not content to introduce a digression; he must also call attention to its digressiveness. Because Dorigen so abruptly dismisses the very question she has just raised, condescendingly leaving it to the wisdom of the "clerkes," her refusal to be philosophically thoroughgoing compels us to linger over the question. In effect, what the dismissal of the question does is to bring the abstract issue into the foreground, forcing a rent in the mimetic seam of the tale so that *theoria*—disinterested philosophical meditation—hovers over the *praxis* of storytelling. But if Chaucer is having his fun with his audience by exaggerating the digressiveness of the digression, it is because his initial refusal to put these lofty questions to any obvious "use" will have the greater dramatic yield. It is only with the tale's denouement that the question of evil is pragmatically—and therefore theoretically—addressed.

One major element that both dramatizes and bridges the gap between speculation and event, between the raising of the question and the outcome of the story, is the Franklin himself, Chaucer's charmingly modest narrator who, in the link, disclaims any storytelling ability ("Colours of retoryk been to me queynte"). Yet if the Franklin's disclaimer smacks of the false modesty of Chaucerian *occupatio*, it is for good reason. As narrator, his own freedom to editorialize, or to let the characters in the tale do their own editorializing, parallels Chaucer's editorial freedom; thus the free motif of the narrator's editorial license creates another level in the story in which thought and action are intertwined. And there is one final extension of form that this Chaucerian narrator involves: *his* philosophical or speculative intrusions are frequently measured against Dorigen's commentaries on her own plight.

By and large, the Franklin uses his editorial freedom in one remarkably consistent way—by subtly but systematically introducing elements of Boethian philosophy, such as the ideals of "gentilleness," "felicitee," and "fredom," motifs which have the effect of mediating the presentation of conflict between characters, placing it in a context of promised concord.[6]

The verbal, ideological, and narratological homage to Boethius of course invokes the most elaborate framing possible: the intertextual framework created by the free motif of systematic allusion. It is interesting, therefore, to compare the narrative strategy of the *Franklin's Tale* with that of Boethius's *Consolation*. What we find is almost a complete reversal of that strategy. In the *Consolation*, there is nothing abstract about Boethius's questioning of universal order. It is intensely personal, spurred on by the hideous predicament of his imprisonment. Philosophy, his guide past the caprices of Fortune, forestalls answering his challenge directly until she can distance him from his preoccupation with his practical bind; once distanced and disinterested, he can take a less niggling view of his own place in the scheme of things. The medicines with which Philosophy cures Boethius are nothing other than explanations of the workings of the universe, and thus Boethius's pragmatic well—being is contingent upon his theoretical understanding. The fascinating emblem of this interconnection is the hem of the dress in which Philosophy first appears to Boethius (and with which she later wipes away his tears). It is imprinted with the letter *P* for *praxis*, above which is a *T* for *theoria*, and between which are "laddres" or steps of understanding by which men climb from the active to the contemplative life.

But whereas in the *Consolation* theoretical understanding is an end in itself, absorbing the pragmatic issues to which theory is addressed, in the *Franklin's Tale*, the free motifs of *theoria* are ultimately answerable to the bound motifs of *praxis*, and finally the two poles become indivisible. Whether they are introduced as the Franklin's glosses on the tale's actions or dialogue or as Dorigen's own interpretations of her plight, it is the Boethian ideals of "trouthe," "gentilesse," and "fredom" that govern the characters' motivations and vanquish the evil embodied in the too palpable black rocks.

A glance at the major source of the *Franklin's Tale*[7] suggests Chaucer's motive for using the rocks motif. In Boccaccio's *Filocolo*, neither the complaint against the rocks on the coast nor

the digression on evil appears. Paralleling Chaucer's unique inclusion of these motifs is the poet's modification of the "damsel's rash promise" of the Italian version. The rash promise of
Dorigen's Italian counterpart has come of the same ironic potential as that of our heroine, but the former's choice is essentially
frivolous; her lover is put to the task of providing her, in January, with a garden blooming as though it were May. The task
Dorigen sets for Aurelius establishes her much more serious
motivation: her concern for her husband's welfare. And more
importantly, it takes up the issue raised in her digression: why
should the rocks exist? Because her speculations have invested
them with metaphysical significance, their presence or removal
will have philosophical implications.

The interpenetration of theory and causality is especially visible
in the Franklin's role in the initial part of the story. First, both in
his link and at the opening of the tale, the Franklin calls attention
to the Breton origin and setting of the tale. Here, even the relatively free authorial choice of setting is bound to the plot, since
"Breytane" provides naturalistic preparation for the appearance of
the "grisly feendly rokkes." More noteworthy still is the Franklin's
commentary on the courtship of Dorigen and Arveragus. He
stresses the knight's willing service of his lady and, counterbalancing this, the readiness of Dorigen's "gentil virtue"—"pitee." While
there is much of conventional courtliness in his suit and her response, the concentration of Boethian terms such as "worthyness,"
"obeysaunce," "pitee," "penance," and "accord" in as the short
span of four lines and the placement of many of these lexical items
in terminal position leaves little doubt as to the Franklin's enthusiasm for his subject and his own commitment to "gentilesse" and
"pitee."

Unskillful as he is, having "couloured" this narrative passage
with such echoes, the Franklin immediately seizes this opportunity to jump off into his own speculations about the nature of love
and to set in motion several paradoxical motifs which, also philosophical in nature, impede the action for thirty–seven lines (761–
98). In validating the romantic love between Dorigen and Arveragus, the narrator presents it in the harmonious terms of the bond of
love. Their love is not "constreyned" by divisive quarrelling over
sovereignty but rather by the constraint of their own free consent.
This paradox, too, is explained by the Franklin in distinctly Boethian terms, terms visible, for example, in Philosophy's statement
that divine love "halt togidres peples joyned with an holy boond,

and knytteth sacrament of mariages . . . and love enditeth lawes to true felawes."[8] The Boethian connection between matrimonial and heavenly law will be quite crucial to the tale's outcome.

But a more local motivation for the Franklin's digression on love presents itself. It is part of the subtle build–up to Dorigen's questioning. Because of the special nature of the marital understanding between Dorigen and Arveragus, her grief at her lord's absence is going to take very special form indeed. In fact, it gives the Franklin one more chance to sneak in a Boethian digression—this time on the pretext of her friends' efforts at "consolation":

> By proces, as ye knowen everichoon,
> Men may so longe graven in a stoon
> Til som figure therinne emprented be.
> So longe han they conforted hire, til she
> Receyved hath, by hope and by resoun,
> The emprentyng of hire consolacioun.   (829–34)

Of course, surreptitiously, Chaucer is also describing the narrative method of the *Franklin's Tale*.

Similarly, the dramatic motivation for Dorigen's scrutiny of Heaven's ways is linked to her marital felicity. But so unobtrusively are we led from Dorigen's innocent wanderings to her fateful defiance that it takes several readings to appreciate fully the finesse of the seemingly casual authorial hand.

At first glance, there seem to be few bound motifs here at all. In its barest terms, the story reduces to the following: because of Dorigen's grief at her lord's absence, her friends suggest that she take walks along the seacoast to distract herself. During her walks, she notices the rocks along the coast, and these seem to her a frightening menace to the safe return of Arveragus's ship. This, in turn, leads to her questioning of the beneficence of the God who has created such perilous natural phenomena.

After closer inspection, however, we observe that the passage begins not with the depiction of one scene, but with the Franklin's presentation of what is actually a composite of several of Dorigen's wanderings, and of her habits of meditation during her walks. The Franklin indicates this with: "Often walketh she" and "another tyme there wolde she sitte and thynke." By thus breaking the pattern of ongoing narrative with the suggestion of a recurrent action, the Franklin prepares us for something more important: Dorigen's psychic obsession with the rocks and all they will come to symbolize to her. But a careful analysis of the rest of the scene reveals an even more anomalous kind of narrative presentation.

For Dorigen's recurrent walks and the recurrent meditations stem from a different kind of causality, one so "loose" as to have the appearance of free association: it is what Dorigen *sees* on the coast that becomes causal. Since this is not superficially apparent, we are told of two of her visions, first, of the ships, which encourages a milder lament, because they remind her of her lord's still absent ship; then, of the rocks, which, because of their horrendous appearance, become the real seed of her fear. The association is as easy as it becomes inevitable. Her glimpse of the rocks suggests that all the elements of nature conspire against her husband's safe return and subverts the very remedy of distraction she had so earnestly been seeking. Because Dorigen's association between the rocks and her lord's absence has both psychic and mimetic validity, we are prepared to believe in the obsessiveness with which the rocks motif appears. "Internal" and "external" motifs are interimplicated.

After such careful preparation, the lines following her glimpse of the "grisly rokkes blake" lead naturally enough to Dorigen's questioning. What is of note in lines 865–93 is that as broad as the implications of her questions get, behind them is her immediate sense of the perilous presence of the rocks; the passionate sting of her interrogation is especially audible in the last part of the questioning:

> An hundred thousand bodyes of mankynde
> Han rokkes slayn, al be they nat in mynde,
> Which mankynde is so fair part of thy werk
> That thou it madest lyk to thyn owene merk.
> Thanne semed it ye hadde a greet chiertee
> Toward mankynde; but how thanne may it bee
> That ye swiche meenes make it to destroyen,
> Whiche meenes do no good, but evere annoyen?
> I woot wel clerkes wol seyn as him leste,
> By argumentz, that al is for the beste,
> Though I ne kan the causes nat yknowe.
> But thilke God that made wynd to blowe
> As kepe my lord! this my conclusion.
> To clerkes lete I al disputison.
> But wolde God that alle thise rokkes blake
> Were sonken into helle for his sake!
> This rokkes sleen myn herte for the feere.   (877–93)

The last three lines of this passage indicate that though Dorigen verbally dismisses the question, it is not because she wishes to forget it but because she cannot forget it. Though the evil which to her seems incapable of mitigation might be perfunctorily deemed "al for the best" by the "clerkes," Dorigen, in her dual role as agent and thinker, is more open to the real intrusiveness of speculation. This lengthy retardation of the action invokes full gamut between speculation and event: the question asked, the question pondered, the absence of an answer, the suppression of the wish for an answer, the question dismissed and the wish to be rid of the reason for the question.

Dorigen's dismissal of the question involves a challenge not only to a generic set of "clerkes" but also, implicitly, to the three kinds of philosophers who might claim to have clearer explanations for the existence of the rocks (apparently a free motif of universal order): the Franklin, Boethius, and the bookish, that is, those who would read of her travails and ponder their implications, albeit at a more comfortable distance. Yet this secure condition of being removed from fictional consequence by no means makes one invulnerable to its effects. For anticipation only conditions the reader to respond more fully to the story's subtlest irony: the revenge of event upon the antefact of speculation. Such engagement also keeps one's attention focused on the fusing of the free motif, the questioning of evil, and the bound motif, the rocks, which are both the occasion for Dorigen's questioning and the instrument of the story's complication.

As I have noted, Jefferson argues that Chaucer differs from Boethius in being more interested in the question of evil itself than in any systematic answer to it.[9] Certainly, for his own narrative purposes, that is the way Chaucer wishes it to appear, not only in having Dorigen so abruptly drop the question but in having the Franklin refrain from commenting at this critical point. In contrast, before Boethius can be satisfied and his remedy achieved, Philosophy has to answer his questions about all the workings of Providence through its agents of Fortune and later of Destiny, and, in relation to them, the function of man's free will. Central to the efficacy of *consolatio* is the gradual change of perspective—the slowly engulfing catharsis of enlightenment to which the Franklin had alluded earlier.

In the *Franklin's Tale*, the catharsis of enlightenment has an entirely different rhythm, appearing and disappearing by turns as we get caught up in the action or seduced into the digressive de-

lights of interpreting it. Essential to this rhythm is an overriding
sense of poetic justice that results from the binding of free motifs
and that balances the claims of speculation at the beginning of the
tale against those of event in the second half and toward the end.
First, Dorigen's testing of divine order is what itself engenders her
being tested. Her obsession with the presence of the rocks is what
leads to her rash promise. In fact, the terms in which she couches
her promise reflect the emotional undertow her speculation has
unleashed:

> "Aurelie," quod she, "by heighe God above
> .   .   .   .
> Looke what day that endelong Britayne
> Ye remoeve alle the rokkes, stoon by stoon,
> That they ne lette ship ne boot to goon.
> .   .   .   .
> Than wol I love yow best of any man,
> Have heer my trouthe, in all that ever I kan."
>
> (989–98)

Symbolically, Dorigen is placing the same impediment before her
lover that now impedes her husband's return; and though her
wording reflects her concern for Arveragus's welfare, it simultaneously places her marriage in jeopardy. When the tregetour converts
the symbolism into "reality," this irony is brought home.

If these inherent ironies of the story are not apparent enough, the
Franklin steps in again in several places to keep them in the fore-
front. For example, he expands upon Dorigen's reunion with her
husband and implies that she has forgotten all about her torment
and her promise. Letting her dwell "in joye and blisse" (1099), he
then turns to the "sike Aurelius," and in describing his lovesick-
ness and his feverish machinations to remove the rocks, the Franklin emphasizes the disproportion between Dorigen's forgetfulness
of and her lover's obsession with them.

But it is Dorigen herself, rather than the Franklin, whose commentary most heightens the sense of poetic justice. When at last
the extensive preparations of the tregetour have the desired effect
and the rocks have "disappeared" from the coast, Dorigen "astoned
stood," taking refuge in her incredulity and protesting, "Wende I
never by possibilitee / That swich a monstre or merveille myghte
be! It is agayns the proces of nature." The protest in these lines has
the impact of startling reversal, for it articulates all the irony of her

first protest: that even in crying out against it, she had axiomatically accepted in the scheme of things the "evil" presence of the rocks; that she had, moreover, made it the cornerstone of her innocence and fidelity. Her former sense of the futility of complaint is all the more rankling now that her objections—which she has long ago forgotten—have been answered. Her very freedom to challenge the order of things has fashioned this insidious logic of compulsion.

It is a logic that Dorigen cannot resist following out to its most obvious conclusion, and Dorigen's lament against fortune and her long catalogue of noble heroines who have resolved upon "deeth" rather than "dishonour" is the last conspicuously digressive element in the tale.[10] Fortune's hand, forestalled, immobilized perhaps, by the very length of this passage, is not so inexorable as Dorigen would have it, and human logic is to be superseded by other, more generous laws.

Both during and after this long passage, where Fate seems most threatening, the Franklin is curiously silent. In stepping back from his interpretative function, he allows Dorigen's misconceptions to reign and his own theorizing role to be superseded by that of Arveragus. Thus the tale's final causes emerge naturally from the confrontation between husband and wife. Perhaps no other moment in Chaucer's poetry so clearly establishes the identity between what happens in fact and what happens in the mind. This scene, vastly different from its corollary in Boccaccio, is much more poignant because of Dorigen's anguish, her directness, and, most of all, Arveragus's comprehension—his willing entry into the realm of idea. The genuineness of their dilemma, the mutuality of their distress, so credible in view of what we have learned of their courtship and marriage, dramatizes a human predicament far more subtle than the marital predicament presented in Boccaccio.[11] Coexistent with Arveragus's sharing of his wife's distress, however, is his faith in the efficacy of "trouthe" and his conviction that the exercise of this virtue is much more important than the ugly practical consequences that would ensue from adherence to logic. Of course, this elevation of *theoria* over *praxis* is no blind optimism either, because it would mean Dorigen's carrying out her word—a prospect that deeply shames Arveragus, however resolute he is. In saying that "trouthe is the hyeste thyng that man may kepe," he implies that to hold to this principle is to move, in action, to the highest level of consciousness. And in encouraging Dorigen to abandon her conventional duty to their marriage vow, he encourages her to look inward for the principle of trouthe, rather than outward, to its apparently evil consequences.

Can the Franklin resist commenting on this speculative leap? Of course not! He seems to have relinquished his editorial role all this while so as to jump in just at the right moment with an interpretative challenge:

> Peraventure an heep of yow, ywis,
> Wol holden hym a lewed man in this
> That he wol putte his wyf in jupartie.
> Herkneth the tale er ye upon hire crie,
> She may have bettre fortune than yow semeth;
> And whan that ye han herd the tale, demeth.
>
> (1493–98)

Taking in both Canterbury pilgrims and readers in its "you," this admonitory intrusion works in several ways: it acknowledges our "interested" curiosity about the outcome of the story, our fixation on causality in the narrower sense, but it also demands a critical alteration of perspective that parallels Arveragus's own; the reader must adopt the disinterested perspective of that most beneficent of comedians whose vision comprehends ultimate causes. And, finally, it thoroughly links the telling of the tale to its "sentence," establishing fiction's power to move its audience into the realm of enlightened action.

We do not have long to wait to see the efficacy of this change in perspective, for if Aurelius had been vulnerable to Dorigen's obsession, he is likewise open to Arveragus's generosity. Among the most moving lines in the tale are those which trace this transformation from lower to higher motives, from *praxis* to *theoria*:

> And in his herte he caughte of this greet routhe,
> Consideryinge the beste on every syde,
> That fro his lust yet were hym levere abyde
> Than doon so heigh a cherlyssh wrecchedness
> Agayns franchise and alle gentilesse.   (1520–24)

To consider the "beste on every syde" is to realize that his practical advantage in this situation would violate the very principles of "franchise and gentilesse" which yield the lady to him. Thus, he too affirms the principle of "trouthe," though he loses every wordly advantage by so doing. And is the tregetour—who is, after all, a "philosophre"—to be outdone? He follows suit, loosing the final bond of obligation in the spirit of gentilesse, as by now, even without the Franklin's hint, we fully expect him to do.

But the Franklin has relinquished his editorial function in this last part of the tale only to redirect us to a more significant stepping back. Though the narrative trajectory of the tale has been completed and conjecture fully embraced by action, the Franklin is once again to draw us back into the dangerous enticements of speculation. With an inimitable grace, this free motif, like Dorigen's musings, is articulated as it could be only by a question: "Which was the mooste fre, as thynketh yow?" Like Philosophy's account, his tale can only side track us into such theoretical detours as the problem of evil and the contradictory claims of freedom and necessity "er that we ferther wende" on our journey. And like all narrators who have accomplished a marriage of the real and the ideal, he must admit—with *true* modesty—"I kan namoore; my tale is at an ende."

U.S. Merchant Marine Academy

NOTES

1. F. N. Robinson, ed., *The Works of Geoffrey Chaucer*, 2nd ed. (Boston: Houghton Mifflin, 1957), p. 137, lines 885–90. All further references to the text are from this edition.

2. Bernard L. Jefferson, *Chaucer and the Consolation of Philosophy of Boethius* (New York: Gordian Press, 1968).

3. In *Russian Formalist Criticism: Four Essays*, trans. and with an introduction by Lee T. Lemon and Marion Reis (Lincoln: University of Nebraska Press, 1965).

4. Ibid., pp. 66–67.

5. Ibid., pp. 68–69.

6. None of these concepts is, of course, the undistilled patrimony of Boethius. Nevertheless, passages in the tale manifesting the *Consolation*'s direct verbal influence (829–34, 865–87, 872–79, 886–87, and 1031) do constitute a reliable index of the Boethian imprint. (I have relied here on Jefferson's tabulations, *Chaucer and the Consolation of Philosophy*, p. 148). They, in turn, reinforce the peculiarly Boethian collocation of 'gentillesse," "trouthe," and "fredom" which one notices in a careful reading of the tale.

7. According to W. F. Bryan and Germaine Dempster, eds., *Sources and Analogues of Chaucer's Canterbury Tales* (New York: Humanities Press, 1958), pp. 377–99.

8. *Boece*, II.M.VIII.

9. Jefferson, *Chaucer and the Consolation of Philosophy,* p. 68 and passim.

10. The scene is one of the few in the *Canterbury Tales* which is comparable to *Troilus and Criseyde* in its delicacy, and is one of the few in literature between a man and a woman which portrays the comprehending mutuality that bridges the sexual divide. Here the impact of the contrast with Boccaccio is crystallized. In the *Filocolo,* the lady, confronted with her "May garden" a few days after her rash promise, goes in, picks the flowers and eats the fruit. She then assures her lover that she will keep her promise but politely asks him to wait until her husband is away from home. Such complicity makes her appearance before her husband that night seem quite manipulative, and the calculation implied is compounded, first by her voicing her lament and suicidal threat in her lord's presence, and then by the fact that, having decked herself out for her appointment, she "bashfully" presents herself to her lover. By contrast, Dorigen's earlier aloneness is reemphasized at this point because her long soliloquy precedes her talk with Arveragus; her directness, chagrin, and helplessness with him are as important to the scene as her husband's generosity.

11. The thrust of Arveragus's advice is once again quite similar to that given in the *Consolation,* which stresses stoicism and self-reliance throughout. The concept of the self as the seat of truth (as well as its Platonic origin) is adumbrated by Dame Philosophy in III.M.11.

Chaucer's Pardoner's Beneficent Lie

Paul C. Bauschatz

*T*he Lie

"When all aspects of the problem of lying have been considered, it is clear that the testimony of the Holy Scriptures advises that one should never lie at all." Thus St. Augustine begins chapter 21, the concluding chapter of *De mendacio.*[1] Lying is not and can never be acceptable to Augustine. The whole question of the lie is a problem for him because he has been confronted by the assertion that there are passages in Scripture where lying is condoned, even justified. Augustine spends a great deal of time in both the *De mendacio* and the *Contra mendacium* examining the matter.[2] He concludes in both treatises that such passages as give rise to the apparent acceptability of lying must "be understood figuratively" *(figurate accipi)* *(De men.* 5); all are expressive of higher truth, which can not be grasped literally. "One should never lie."

The lie as Augustine defined it, and as it has remained since his time, is a kind of falsehood based primarily upon intent, which may or may not involve objective untruth as well: "In reality, the fault of the person who tells a lie consists in his desire to deceive in expressing his thought"*(De men.* 3, pp. 55–56).[3] One may utter falsehood *(falsum dicere)* without lying provided that one speaks from a firm belief in truth of what one erroneously says. The utterance is false, but it is not a lie. Further: "it happens that a person who is actually lying [speaking with the intent to deceive] may say what is true, if he believes that what he says is false, yet offers it as true, even if the actual truth be just what he says" *(De men.* 3, p. 55).[4] Neither true speaking nor lying can be accidental. The intent of the speaker to speak truth *(verum dicere)* or to deceive *(mentire)* underlies all speaking. When the intent to speak truth is imperfect, or when it is imperfectly carried out (the act of lying can never be

19

"imperfect" in this way), the resulting utterance will be classified by Augustine as "false." False speaking without lying can take a number of forms: It may occur in "harmless" jokes or word play *(iocis mendacia) (De men. 2).*

It also occurs when "some kind of speech, frequently repeated and memorized, flows out of the speaker's mouth while he is thinking of something else . . . ; or, unintentionally, and by a slip of the tongue, some words are blurted out instead of others, so that in this case too, the words which are heard are not signs of what is in our mind" *(De mag.* 13 (42), pp. 56–57).[5] In all these cases, the speaker either is not entirely in control of what is said or imperfectly represents the relationship between language and what it expresses.[6] Augustine is, however, always careful to differentiate all these possibilities from lying. Lying must be informed by the will to deceive, and there can be no lie when that will is lacking.

By definition, the lie is excluded from Scripture. Scripture is the expression of God's will, which neither deceives nor misleads. God does not lie; Scripture does not lie. Man's responsibility to God's book and to His work is such that he must strive to understand God's discourse and imitate it in his own speech. Augustine is always concerned with expanding man's understanding of the Scriptures. This concern leads him to consider the nature of man's speech too. As man attends to God's word, which never lies at all, he learns as well of his own speech that "one should never lie at all." Augustine is interested in the semantic as well as the ethical dimension of language use. With resect to lying, he is interested both in the ethos of the liar and in the way he wants his words to be understood. Because he most directly concerns himself with problems of the will, Augustine is most likely to deal with lying from the point of view of the liar rather than from the point of view of one who must decode the lie.[7] Man's discourse must imitate God's, and God's discourse is an unqualifiedly direct presentation of His true and benevolent will. A man wholly attendant upon God need not worry about the lie at all. When we read Scripture, we need only concern ourselves with understanding it fully. It is only when we become overly concerned with the nature of man's speech that the question of how to decipher the true from the false becomes problematical. The problem of secular lying does not engage Augustine centrally. If we pay attention to the truth, we will, of necessity, avoid the lie.

Augustine is concerned with what St. Anselm seven hundred years later would call *Summa Veritas,* "the Supreme Truth." Augustine, in his search to understand the nature of such a Supreme *Veritas*, was concerned that it be left unviolated by any thing of or pertaining to *mendax*, which some men incorrectly had attributed to it. For Augustine, *mendax* is totally of the created world. This is true also for Anselm, but for him, the question of the nature of all *veritas* (Supreme and otherwise) *is* an issue. In particular, Anselm is ever eager to detect extensions of the Supreme *Veritas* into the creation itself. Thus, Anselm's *De veritate* examines the extent to which all aspects of the creation are suffused with rectitude, his term for what might be called the "created nature of truth." For Anselm, it is this created *veritas*, not *mendax*, which is of primary importance. There is in all of Anselm's work an implicit belief in the truth of reason, in the truth of reasonable logic, and in the true rectitude of the language used to make such logical and reasonable statements. In this way, Anslem has broken "in a pretty radical way ... with St. Augustine and the whole Augustinian tradition. ... But of course there is not the slightest evidence to suppose that St. Anselm was consciously parting company with St. Augustine, nor that Anselm's contemporaries saw him as an innovator on this question."[8] It is true that both Augustine and Anselm place faith in a primary position, but Anselm's fame as a thinker and scholar derives from his continual attention to the discovery of *veritas essentiae rerum*, "the truth in the being of things."[9] It is ever the delight of Anselm's will to be in the process of reasoning, to be evolving an ever larger understanding of the nature of things. This process seems not to have interested Augustine overly much. He grows impatient with it and eventually finds it limiting and noisome, a constantly present emblem of man's imperfect, created nature.[10] Though Anselm always defers to the Supreme Truth, he labors with pleasure through and in the nature of language, of action, and of things themselves to find every morsel of *veritas* therein. He has been called the father of scholasticism, and it is hard to think of the great achievements of the fourteenth century, the *Summas*, for example, or the whole school of speculative grammarians (the Modistae), without his example.[11]

Anselm's logical bent and grammatical training make human language a primary instrument in his search for *veritas* as well as one of the targets upon which he focuses his analytical eye. Discussions of the nature of language, both incidental and central, turn up everywhere. The *De grammatico* is largely concerned with a demonstration that both being and action and the predication of being and action are "real." The *Philosophical Fragments* deal directly with

The contradictory natures of (A) and (C), (B) and (D) are clear, as is the contrary nature of (A) and (B), although we might not wish nowadays to call them "contraries." What proves to be most useful for Anselm's logical progression is the semantic equivalence established through consentients, that (A) "is sometimes used in place of" (D), and vice versa. Consentients provide a propositional or logical equivalent to the grammatical concept of synonymy. Synonymy equates the "significance" of a predication at word level, but consentients operate within what any medieval scholar would have called logic rather than grammar. Anselm is most interested not in the meaning (at word level) of the verb *facere* but in the uses to which it can be put in predicating causes. The fact that *facere* sometimes predicates or makes reference to actions which seem merely to happen (to do) and sometimes predicates actions redolent of immediate causality (to cause, to force, to make someone do something) is not of great interest to Anselm, nor is he overly concerned with the possibilities of replacing *facere* in any context with any one of a number of possible synonymous verbs. Rather, he wishes to codify the kinds of relationships in which different kinds of verb phrases or sentences utilizing *facere* can signify the *same* causes.

Although this four-way scheme of relationships among contraries, contradictories, and consentients is too simple to catch many of the nuances of Anselm's thought, it does indicate the way in which his mind approaches the discovery of truth in action and in things within the created world. He is especially delighted when he discovers some paradoxical appearance among different aspects of what he considers to be similar things. *De veritate* is especially interesting from just this point of view. In it, Anselm examines the apparent paradoxes which result from man's attempts to come to grips with what seems to be the contradictory nature of *veritas*. In chapter eight, for example, he is concerned with finding a reasonable explanation for the presence of evil action in the world. The disciple begins the chapter by asking "how can we say truthfully that whatever is ought to be, since there are many evil deeds which certainly ought not to be?"[15] The teacher, after establishing that "nothing at all *is* except by God's causing it or permitting it," concludes:

So the same thing both ought and ought not to be. It ought to be since it is permitted wisely and well by God, without whose permission it could not have happened. Yet, with respect to him by whose evil will it is committed (*concipitur*),

it ought not to be. In this way, then, the Lord Jesus ought not
to have undergone death because He alone [among men] was
innocent; and no one ought to have inflicted death upon Him;
nevertheless, He ought to have undergone death because He
wisely and graciously and usefully willed to undergo it. For in
many ways the same thing admits in different respects of
opposites. (De ver. 8, p. 87)[16]

The differing linguistic approaches to the "same" event each give
us some truth relevant to our understanding of the whole reality
toward which our will should move. In assimilating this complex-
ity, we are in the process of evolving incrementally that greater
understanding. Nothing could be further from Augustine's
thought. He would have needed say no more than "it ought to be
since it is permitted wisely and well by God." Nor would he have
seen the need to modify the predication by "wisely and well."

The Beneficent Lie

If, as Augustine has told us, we are to act rightly by aligning our
will with God's will, we are going to get in trouble with Anselm's
logic.[17] We can see it coming in the short passage about the Crucifixion just quoted. Anselm carefully keeps his contrary actions
unopposed by stating them in terms which discourage opposition:
"Jesus ought not to have undergone death because He . . . was innocent . . . ; nevertheless, He ought to have undergone death because He willed to undergo it." If we examine the action from the
point of view of the "death dealer," those who either should or
should not cause His death, rather than from the will of Jesus, we
discover that the logical relations among these cases contrast, on
the one hand, those who follow God's will by refusing to kill the
innocent and, by its diagonal contradictory, those who do not follow God's will by not refusing to kill Jesus. On the other hand,
over and against this, we have another case, the "contrary" case:
those who must, of necessity, follow God's will by killing the Lord
Jesus since it is His will that He die. (The contradictory alternative
to this, that refusal to take part in the killing of Jesus is against
God's will, does not appear but is logically implied as well.) Thus,
since the Crucifixion is a willed act, those who participate actively
in it can very well be seen to do so in accordance with God's will;
those who know God's will best should be those most likely to
take part. Here's trouble indeed.

Anselm never considers this particular question. It is, in a very real sense, unthinkable for him. His four-cornered logical model causes no problems when he examines the interrelations among actions within the created world, as his "neutral" examination of the predicational relations for the verb *facere* illustrates. For him, as for Augustine, matters of the Supreme Truth differ qualitatively from matters of the created world. Scriptural matters have their own *Veritas* not given over to the problems inherent in the *veritas* within creation. Why then has Anselm, in the passage just examined, mixed, perhaps inadvertently, these two discourses: the discourse of Scripture, or of faith, with the logical discourse of human understanding? In one sense, it provides a way of elevating human discourse to show how it interacts with Scripture, and Anselm wants always to make the move from *veritas* to *Veritas*. The productive exploitation of exactly this kind of logically derived paradox will mark much of the scholarly and literary output of the centuries following Anselm. It is this same logical move which informs the early fifteenth-century English lyric "Bless the Time the Apple was Taken!" This short poem (eight lines) develops in its first four lines the context of Adam's bondage in hell prior to his release through Christ's sacrifice. Adam has lain there in bondage four thousand winters for eating the fatal apple. However,

> Ne hadde þe appil take ben, þe appil taken ben,
> ne hadde neuer our lady a ben heuene qwen;
> Blyssid be þe tyme that appil take was,
> þer-fore we mown syngyn, "deo gracias!"   (5–8)[18]

The progression in the poem to its perception of the *felix culpa* expresses maximally the kind of logical relation implicit in Anselm's model. It is useful for making that which appears to be evil turn out to be a variation of that which is good.

When we move from an examination of actions within the created world to the examination of the predication of these actions and to the relations among word and will and action, we discover that the same peculiar fourth corner of Anselm's logical model suggests itself. As Augustine has already made very clear, "a person is to be judged as lying or not lying according to the intention of his own mind, not according to the truth or falsity of the matter itself" (*De men.* 3, p. 55).[19] Hence, to place one's will (intention) in direct concord with the will of God and to speak directly to that will is to tell the truth.[20] Second, to think or to believe that one's will is in accord with God's will and to speak to that will is to speak *either* the truth *(verum dicere)* (when the speaker's will *is* in conformity with God's will) *or* falsehood *(falsum dicere)* (when the will of the speaker does not conform to God's will). Third, to take one's will and to turn it intentionally from the truth of God's will is to lie *(mentire)*. All this is clear from Augustine. These three cases, when plotted on the four-cornered logical model, create a position for a fourth possibility. It will vary, of course, depending upon how one wishes to see the exact "logical" nature of the relations among true "merry" speech, falsehood (jangling), and lying. With respect to the formulation outlined above, the model allows for a fourth kind of speech, in which man's will is turned consciously from God's but with articulatory force such that it produces speech and action in congruence with the "truer" or "higher" nature of things (fig. 2).

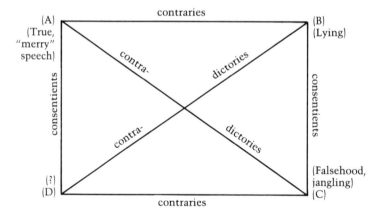

It is the contradictory of the lie, because it articulates that which is false in intent but to an "inappropriate" (i.e., a "not false") end; it is the contrary of falsehoods (which lead to bad or "false" ends) since both jangling and lying lead to "bad," "evil" ends inappropriate to Right Will. Point (D) on the diagram is also consentient with point (A), true speech. It provides the double negative of truth, and, as such, it proves "positive." Point (D) provides us with what we might call the "beneficent" lie. The idea of any kind of "beneficent" lie is flatly rejected by Augustine. It is not one of the logical options which Anselm pursues either, but to leave such an option lying around is to invite someone to pick it up.

The Pardoner's Beneficent Lie

The Pardoner on Chaucer's Canterbury pilgrimage has clearly picked the option up, and he offers it as one of the central principles of his *modus operandi*.[21] That he is a liar is not new; he is one of the greatest liars in the whole of English literature, but his claim is greater:

> Thus kan I preche agayn that same vice
> Which that I use, and that is avarice.
> But though myself be gilty in that synne,
> Yet kan I maken oother folk to twynne
> From avarice, and soore to repente.   (C. 427–31)[22]

This is not the speech of a typical liar, as Augustine has defined him, whose heart is double, "that is, two-fold in its thinking: one part consisting of that knowledge which he knows or thinks to be true, yet does not so express it; the other part consisting of that knowledge which he knows or thinks to be false, yet expresses as true" (*De men.* 3, p. 55).[23] If we take the Pardoner's words as directly as we can (and this, with the Pardoner, is a difficult—if not a dangerous—undertaking), we can see him as lacking the heartfelt duplicity discussed by Augustine. He asserts as a matter of faith the forthrightness and singleness of his purpose: through sin, he saves.

The logic of the whole of the Pardoner's prologue and of his following tale explores fully the predicational options inherent in Anselm's four-cornered model. His assertion of his beneficent lying is but one of several different kinds of assertions his discourse makes, but what makes the Pardoner's procedure peculiar is the odd tack he uses to present these options. They appear in what we might take to be the reverse of their traditional or expected order; we would surely expect him to begin with what we have been calling option (A), true speech. True speech does not really appear until the Pardoner has plunged us directly and fully into the *exemplum* of his sermon concerning the fates of the three rioters who set out to murder Death. Prior to that, in the prologue which frames the *exemplum*, the Pardoner gives us a series of statements expressive of his intellectual and moral sense of himself. None of these is very obviously expressive of "truth" as we expect it to be. But the presentation of these other kinds of speech provides him a context in which we must interpret the nature of the following tale.

He begins:

> "Lordynges," quod he, "in chirches whan I preche,
> I peyne me to han an hauteyn speche,
> And rynge it out as round as gooth a belle,
> For I kan al by rote that I telle.   (329–32)

The fact that the Pardoner concerns himself foremost with the
form of his speech presents us with a situation in which we recognize speech much like Augustine's "falsehood." The Pardoner,
in these his very first words upon the subject, seems to be giving us
a statement of belief in which he asserts that the *form*, "round as
gooth a belle," is of greater significance than the content of his
"speche." In line 332, we learn that, indeed, the "content" of this
speech lies elsewhere; it has been learned "al by rote."[24] The Pardoner plays his sermon as if he were playing a victrola, and in the
playing he is more concerned with the quality of reproduction than
with the particular record he has chosen to be played. True speech
does not operate this way. To dissociate content from the act of
speaking is to jangle. The simile he provides for his preaching,
"round as gooth a belle," seems appropriate to this focus of surface
over substance. Later, in returning to the same issue, he expresses
his procedure thus:

> I preche so as ye han herd bifoore,
> And telle an hundred false japes moore.
> Than peyne I me to strecche forth the nekke,
> And est and west upon the peple I bekke,
> As dooth a dowve sittynge on a berne.   (393–97)

Birds, here a "dowve," provide for us directly the most immediate
natural analog to human jangling, which the bell earlier had begun
to suggest.

He jangles on by rote and tells his "japes," a convenient way of
suggesting that what he is doing in his preaching is not serious.
They are merely "jocose lies, which have never been considered as
real lies, since both in the verbal expression and in the attitude of
the one joking such lies are accompanied by a very evident lack of
intention to deceive" (*De men.* 2, p. 54).[25] Augustine explicitly
denies such japes any relation to the problem of real lying, and the
Pardoner's term attempts similar dismissal. The "hundred false
japes" he has referred to in line 394, however, are tales told to his

"lewed" listeners about "bulles of popes," "cristal stones," the shoulder bone of a "hooly Jewes sheep," and so forth—a plenty of "holy" materials and relics, but, in all probability, *not* God's. And, contrary to Augustine's definition of the jape, the intent to deceive is not lacking here:

> Of avarice and of swich cursednesse
> Is al my prechyng, for to make hem free
> To yeven hir pens, and namely unto me. (400–02)

All this preaching is not, we must note, to make those who hear him "free" from sin and to "give" their pence to the Pardoner as a sign of contrition and as a token of their good will so that he, as God's vicar (which we have surely begun to suspect that he is not, anyway), may do God's work; on the contrary, the Pardoner's

> entente is nat but for to wynne,
> And nothyng for correccioun of synne.
> I rekke nevere, whan that they been beryed,
> Though that hir soules goon a-blakeberyed! (403–06)

No. His intent *is* to deceive, and he is lying to these "lewed peple" in Augustine's typical, traditional way.

From jangling and lying it is but an easy jump across to their respective contrary and contradictory, to the beneficent lie:

> For certes, many a predicacioun
> Comth ofte tyme of yvel entencioun. (407–08)

Such predications should, through their evil intent, become lies directly, but the Pardoner has in mind something more negative. The kind of logical predication he is leading us toward is suggested first in the linguistically involuted statement about how he controls anyone to whom he preaches who might be unwilling to accept his preaching:

> Thanne wol I stynge hym with my tonge smerte
> In prechyng, so that he shal nat asterte
> To been defamed falsly.   (413–15)

The doubly negative pattern of this utterance is carried over logically into the full enunciation of the beneficent lie which follows it:

> Thus kan I preche agayn that same vice
> Which that I use, and that is avarice.
> But though myself be gilty in that synne,
> Yet kan I maken oother folk to twynne
> From avarice, and soore to repente.   (427–31)

The Pardoner has provided himself with a blasphemous and outra-
geous context in which to tell his tale. And tell it he does, and very
well too, so well, in fact, that we and everyone else who has heard
it or read it have been drawn into it just as were those "lewed
peple" who "loven tales olde," for whom he apparently learned it
all "by rote." The telling of the tale is a great success. It is only
toward the end of the tale proper, around line 903, that we begin to
become aware once again of the context in which the Pardoner is
speaking. Usually later, around line 919 (or perhaps earlier, maybe
around line 915), readers begin to suspect that the Pardoner has
moved from his "rote" sermon to some other kind of speaking. He
seems to be returning to the context established by his prologue,
the logical context in which the *exemplum* we have just enjoyed
has been told. But from which of the possible predicational options
is he speaking? Is he jangling again? Is he lying? Is he lying benevo-
lently, attempting to lead us aright at the expense of his own salvation? We are at a loss to tell. The text itself seems to go out of its
way to make any firm decision on our part difficult. We are lost in
a wood of predicational possibilities. Nor does it help us when the
Pardoner tells us finally:

> And Jhesu Crist, that is oure soules leche,
> So graunte yow his pardoun to receyve,
> For that is best; I wol yow nat deceyve.   (916–18)

   The Pardoner's speech has illustrated for us that he may speak in
conformity with his will or in a manner totally dissociated from
his will. He allows us everywhere all the possibilities for interpreting the intentions predicated in each act of speech. Likewise, he
encourages us to look for all the possibilities as we attempt to
discover his intention. As a result, even the clear, straightforward-
sounding affirmation of lines 916–18 becomes suspect. Nor can we
interpret "I wol yow nat deceyve" wisely and well.

Chaucer's Pardoner's Beneficent Lie

The Pardoner is a fiction, a part of the longer fiction of the Canterbury pilgrimage which Chaucer has given us. The Pardoner's dis-

course within that fiction is, as we read it, not a fiction. Our responses to it are immediate and real. If it is true, as Chaucer seems fond of telling us, "that al that writen is, / To oure doctrine it is ywrite" (Group B², 4631–32), what is doctrinal in the words which he has given to the Pardoner? There seems, in fact, to be no doctrine in them. In the sense of Scriptural doctrine, as St. Paul explicitly makes it and as Augustine would surely have interpreted St. Paul's words, there is none. At best, the Pardoner can claim to be the anti-priest of a counterscripture, but within the more ordinary Scriptural context, he is not even a "good" devil. On the other hand, if we take doctrine to be something that might be learned, *anything* that might be learned, we can see our perplexity at the whole of the Pardoner's prologue and tale as itself an example of learning. Our problems in reading the Pardoner's discourse suggest that no language among men, no matter how clever, how convincing, or how competent, may be taken at face value. We are, each of us, fallible; our fallibility leads us to credulity and to skepticism. The discourse given to the Pardoner logically interweaves all possible relations among truths and falsehoods. The rational model, which formed the basis of the scholastic enterprise of the thirteenth and fourteenth centuries and which offered so many viable options for examining and codifying human understanding, has become, in the words of the Pardoner, a weapon for the destruction of that very understanding. Where everything can mean itself, its consentient, its contradictory, or its contrary, nothing can mean anything. All language is a trap.

For both Augustine and Anselm, such problems did not arise. For them, human language differed essentially from the language of Scripture. The nature of discourse among men about created matters was always distinct from that discourse which attempted to discover the nature of spiritual truth. For Augustine, created truth and Scriptural truth were different in kind. That reason could lead to faith he would acknowledge, but his interest is always upon the fullest understanding of faith. In this, logic is a useful instrument only, and understanding, in its fullest sense, is reached only with the move to faith. For Anselm, the division between reason and faith, small *veritas* and Supreme *Veritas*, is less distinct but still present, and logic does not—cannot—question the primacy of Supreme Truth. For Chaucer's Pardoner, however, what Anselm would call the Supreme Truth has become only one aspect of the four-cornered logical model. It is merely one variant, one part of "true speaking." As such, it is consentient with the double negative of the beneficent lie. The Pardoner has, through his logic, provided for himself a position from which he can proclaim himself in possession of a "truth" whose value is, at least, the equivalent of God's or, at best, truer than God's. He implies that he knows more about the nature of things and about the greater realities of human expression than God does. From the Pardoner's point of view, God has limited Himself to speaking within only one small corner of all linguistic possibility. As a result, God speaks only a staid, direct truth. The Pardoner has a much greater linguistic area over which to operate. His discourse suggests that he has opened out new frontiers of human understanding. In this, he is the predecessor of much later literary usurpers of divine prerogative: Satan in William Blake's reading of Milton's *Paradise Lost* or Judas in Nikos Kazantzakis's *The Last Temptation of Christ*.

Within the fiction of *The Canterbury Tales* as a whole, however, the Pardoner's assertion fails. We are not sure why. The end of the *Pardoner's Tale* is enigmatic.[26] In concluding his tale, the Pardoner says strange things and makes strange linguistic moves which suggest either a lack of control over his own discourse or a desire on his part to destroy the very premises upon which he has predicated the whole telling of his tale. Why is he doing this? We do not know. What are his motivations? We do not know those either. From everything we have been able to learn about the Pardoner and from what we have been told before the conclusion of the tale, we realize that his motivations and his reasons could be just about anything. All possibilities are possible. What we learn explicitly is that Harry Bailly responds with anger after the Pardoner has offered him a chance to "kisse the relikes everychon." Readers generally approve Harry Bailly's response; the Pardoner has got what he deserves. But this surely cannot be right—that the appropriate, positive, and doctrinal end of any discourse would lead to anger. That a problematical discourse like the Pardoner's should be rejected we accept, but that it should lead those who hear it to sin, that cannot be right. Harry Bailly's anger breeds yet more; the Pardoner becomes angry too:

> This Pardoner answerede nat a word;
> So wrooth he was, no word ne wolde he seye. (956–57)

His silence is as enigmatic and as disturbing as Iago's at the end of *Othello*, and the Knight's solution, having Harry Bailly and the Pardoner kiss and make up, does little to alleviate our own dis-ease.

The Pardoner is Chaucer's fiction, and his discourse is Chaucer's artifact. The questions which it raises work back against the whole fiction in which Chaucer has plunged us. The various kinds of tests to which Chaucer has put human understanding in the discourse of the Canterbury pilgrimage are taken to their fullest extreme in the Pardoner's prologue and tale. On the surface, the Pardoner speaks with the same kind of plenitude that informs the tale of the Nun's Priest: each teller uses variety and contradiction and multiplicity of reference to give his tale intellectual depth and interest. Each teller utilizes confusion and profusion as essential elements in the creation of a complex context. The distinction between the two, however, seems to reside in the will of each speaker. The orientation of the Nun's Priest's will is never in question. When he asks us to sort out from the abundance which he has given us "the fruyt" from "the chaf," we engage in the task willingly, and as readers we are rewarded. But with the Pardoner, we don't even know how to begin to sort. Everything might be fruit, or chaff, or both, or neither.

The *reasonable* basis upon which human understanding has been predicated has been so fully utilized by the Pardoner that the whole ground upon which a discourse of understanding might be built has been reduced to sand—shifty, unstable, and untrustworthy. Where everything is true, it doesn't matter what one says. As a result, even words which have the ring of Scripture sound suspect: *Is* Christ's pardon really the best? The Pardoner says so, but he has also said much else. What is the validity of what he says? Maybe, just maybe, he knows more about Christ's pardon than we have suspected. Why *is* it the best? What are the *reasons?* Maybe there's something about Christ's pardon that he isn't telling us. Our suspicions increase with the Pardoner's very next words: "But, sires, o word forgat I in my tale" (919). Has he forgotten to tell us something else about Christ's pardon? We listen.

Reason becomes a danger without the check of Scriptural authority. The silence at the end of the *Pardoner's Tale* is a Scriptural void and a void of human discourse as well. There is no longer space for word or Word, *veritas* or *Veritas*. We must accept this silence directly, or we must turn from it to the assurance of the discourse of faith. True prayer is the only alternative to the Pardoner's sullen silence. If the Pardoner's performance has given us any benefit, it is that we must believe and that we must act directly and in accordance with that belief. Chaucer, however, in giving us the Pardoner's prologue and tale, has not presented us with this kind of direct accordance. Rather, within the logical model of understanding, he has given us a consentient alternative to direct true speaking. Finally, the fiction of the tale telling asserts that this alternative is only an illusion, an illustration of the failure of all indirect discourse. Chaucer's Pardoner replicates in a particularly disturbing and forceful way the weakness of all fictionalizing, of the whole process of tale telling upon which the Canterbury pilgrimage is itself predicated. Can the value of the Pardoner's speaking lie in his reifying for us the self-destructive nature of a human understanding dominated by logic and unchecked by faith? If so, the Pardoner's only conclusion is silence.[27] Likewise, all the tales within the fiction will end in silence; it is their only escape from their own fictions.

The end of *The Canterbury Tales* as we have them proves problematical for most modern readers. We generally have difficulties with the shift which is so observable in the movement from Group H of the tales (the *Manciple's Prologue* and *Tale*) through the beginning of Group I (the *Parson's Prologue* and *Tale*), which begins with Harry Bailly speaking but turns quickly to the Parson. the *Parson's Tale* and the "retracciouns" of "the makere of this book" mark for all of us a real shift in the nature of the discourse in which we have been till this point employed. Chaucer has made the ending of "this book" palpably direct. It concludes by asking us to participate directly in its own final consideration of the value of its own fictions. It demonstrates that "lies . . . should either be avoided in right action or be confessed in penitence. But, they should not, though they abound unhappily in our living, be increased by our teaching" (*Contra men.* 21, p. 178).[28]

University of Maine at Orono

NOTES

1. "Elucet itaque discussis omnibus nihil aliud illa testimonia scripturarum monere nisi numquam esse omnino mentiendum" (*De mendacio*, XXI [42], p. 463). Latin quotations are from Sancti Aureli Augustini, *Corpus scriptorum ecclesiasticorum latinorum*, ed. Iosephus Zycha, vol. 41, sect. V, pars III (Vienna: F. Tempsky, 1890). *De mendacio* and *Contra mendacium* are both included in this volume: *De mendacio*, pp. 411–66; *Ad consentium contra mendacium*, pp. 467–528. The English translation quoted in the text (and cited by chapter and page number) is from

Saint Augustine, *Treatises on Various Subjects*, vol. 14, in *The Fathers of the Church*, ed. Roy Joseph Deferrari et al., vol. 16 (Washington, D. C.: The Catholic University of America Press, 1952), p. 107. Translations of both *De mendacio* and *Contra mendacium* are included in this volume: *De mendacio* as "Lying," trans. Sister Mary Sarah Muldowney, pp. 47–110; *Contra mendacium* as "Against Lying," trans. Harold B. Jaffee, pp. 113–79. These two texts are not among the treatises of St. Augustine most widely read in modern times. As noted by Marcia L. Colish several years ago in "St. Augustine's Rhetoric of Silence Revisited" (*Augustinian Studies*, 9 [1978], 15–24), in which an analysis of these two texts figures significantly in her argument, "the *De mendacio* and *Contra mendacium* have excited very little attention on the part of Augustine scholars" (p. 16). More recently, they have received further consideration in two places: first, in a paper given by Eugene Vance, "Speech-Act Theory in the Middle Ages: Augustine and Chaucer on Lying," at the 96th Annual Convention of the MLA in New York, on 28 December 1981; second, in Marcia L. Colish, "The Stoic Theory of Verbal Signification and the Problem of Lies and False Statements from Antiquity to St. Anselm" (*Archeologie du signe*, ed. Lucie Brind'Amour and Eugene Vance [Toronto: Pontifical Institute of Medieval Studies, 1982], pp. 17–43).

2. In the *De mendacio*, eleven chapters of twenty-one are fully given over to it; in the *Contra mendacium*, fourteen chapters of twenty-one. These are, generally, the longer chapters of each treatise. It should be kept in mind, however, that the major point of interest in the *Contra mendacium* is the question, raised by the Priscillianists, of whether the true faith might be furthered by its members lying in order to infiltrate, both intellectually and physically, the domain of heretics.

3. "Culpa uero mentientis est in enuntiando animo suo fallendi cupiditas" (*De men.* III [3], p. 415). In all the treatises in which Augustine explicitly discusses lying and how it is to be distinguished from true speech, the speaker's intention is a necessary element. Besides being the central concern of the *De mendacio* and *Contra mendacium*, discussions of lying figure importantly in *De magistro*, in *De doctrina christiana*, and, to a somewhat lesser degree, in *De trinitate*. In *De mendacio* and in *De magistro*, the presence of intention to deceive is sufficient to define lying. In *Contra mendacium* and in *De doctrina christiana*, intent to deceive is necessary but not sufficient to define lying. Since these last two texts deal directly with matters of interpreting Scripture and propagating the faith, elements necessary to the true understanding of the nature of faith and of Scripture enter the definitions in a significant way. Since the nature of the truth in Scripture is absolute and one's "true" orientation to it must likewise be absolute, any reading of it which fails to realize its (Scripture's) intent lies: "Whoever, therefore, thinks that he understands the divine Scriptures or any part of them so that it does not build the double love of God and of our neighbor does not understand it at all. Whoever finds a lesson there useful to the building of charity, even though he has not said what the author may be shown to have intended in that place, has not been deceived, nor is he lying in any way" (*De doctrina christiana*, Book I, XXXVI [40], p. 30, in Saint Augustine, *On Christian Doctrine*, trans. D. W. Robertson, Jr. [New York: The Liberal Arts Press, 1958]). "Quisquis igitur scripturas diuinas uel quamlibet earum partem intellexisse sibi uidetur, ita ut eo intellectu non aedificet istam geminam caritatem dei et proximi, nondum intellexit. Quisquis uero talem inde sententiam duxerit, ut huic aedificandae caritati sit utilis, nec tamen hoc dixerit, quod ille quem legit eo loco sensisse probabitur, non perniciose fallitur nec omnino mentitur" (Sancti Aurellii Augustini, *De doctrina christiana*, Liber primus, XXXVI [40], p. 29, in *Corpus chris-*

tianorum, series latina, 32 [Aurelii Augustini, *Opera, pars* IV, 1] [Turnholt: Brepols, 1962]). For the various definitions of lying to be found in St. Augustine's work, I am much indebted to Marcia L. Colish, especially to her essay "The Stoic Theory of Verbal Signification."

4. "Ut possit uerum dicere mentiens, si putat falsum esse et pro uero enuntiat, quamuis reuera ita sit, ut enuntiat" (*De men.,* III [3], p. 415). Augustine makes this kind of argument almost exclusively when he is dealing with man's own speech (as here and in much of *De magistro*). It is not typical of his arguments about the nature of lying in texts that are more directly concerned with matters of Scriptural exegesis.

5. Saint Augustine, *The Teacher, the Free Choice of the Will, Grace and Free Will,* trans. Robert P. Russell, in *The Fathers of the Church,* ed. Roy Joseph Deferrari et al., vol. 59 (Washington, D. C.: The Catholic University of America Press, 1968). "Cum aut sermo memoriae mandatus et saepe decursus alia cogitantis ore funditur ... aut cum alia pro aliis verba praeter voluntatem nostram linguae ipsius errore prosiliunt; nam hic quoque non earum rerum signa, quas in animo habemus, audiuntur" (*De mag.,* XIII [42], p. 51, in *Corpus scriptorum ecclesiasticorum latinorum,* 77 [Sancti Aureli Augustini, *Opera,* sect. VI, *pars* IV: *De magistro,* ed. Guenther Weigel] [Vienna: Hoelder, Pichler, Tempsky, 1961]).

6. Augustine's "false speaking" corresponds closely to the Middle English term *jangling.* A variety of noun forms, in addition to the verb *jangle,* were in common usage in the fourteenth century (*jangle, jangler, janglerie, jangling,* etc.). All derive their meanings from the verb. According to the *MED* (*Middle English Dictionary*), ed. Sherman M. Kuhn and John Reidy, Part J.1 (Ann Arbor: The University of Michigan Press, 1969), pp. 368–71, *jangle* and its derivatives refer, on the one hand, to bird calls (chattering or twittering) and, on the other, to human speech. In order of descending frequency, the uses of *jangle* in human contexts refer to chatter or idle talking, chiding or nagging, grumbling, arguing, or contradicting. In the contexts where arguing or contradicting are central, the tone is generally ironic or dismissive. The OED suggests that *jangle* is "often applied contemptuously to ordinary speaking." All references to human jangling in the *MED* are negatively tinged. Some have more than a tinge of the negative, as in the following from *Piers Plowman: The B Version,* ed. George Kane and E. Talbot Donaldson (London: University of London, The Athlone Press, 1973). At the Last Supper, Christ says:

> "I am sold þoruჳ [som] of yow; he shal þe tyme rewe
> That euer he his Saueour solde for siluer or ellis."
> Iudas iangled perayein, ac Iesus hym tolde
> It was hymself sooþly and seide "tu dicis."   (16: 142–45)

"Jangle," in line 144, clearly refers immediately to contradiction, but he is denying Holy Truth here. We know he is lying, as the occurrence of "sooþly" in line 145 makes explicit. One may understate the seriousness of a lie by using *jangle* to refer to it for ironic effect. All readers or hearers of *Piers Plowman* know this, and this knowledge renders the irony apparent. From the point of the hearer or reader, however, not all contexts present the immediate information necessary for interpreting the full import of the word's use. Jangling and lying are alike when we are unsure of the intent which gives rise to them. All we can know for sure is that the speech has gone wrong. When we set up a hierarchy of semantic marks to associate lying and jangling, we discover that lying is the marked form: it *always* makes reference to speech gone wrong through wrong intent. Jangling is neutral with respect to intention in this sense. It is only within the paradigm of "infelicitous" speech that the meaningful opposition of jangling to lying occurs.

7. The problems of decoding lies do surface occasionally in Augustine's work, usually in moments where he seems to approach exasperation: "I have no doubt whatever that the words of truthful men are an attempt and a sort of pledge to reveal the thoughts of the speaker, and that they would succeed in this, as all agree, if only liars were not allowed to speak" (*De mag.* 13 [42], p. 56). "Nam nullo modo ambigo id conari verba veracium et id quodam modo profiteri, ut animus loquentis appareat, quod obtinerent omnibus concedentibus, si loqui mentientibus non liceret" (*De mag.* XIII [42], p. 51). Augustine's turn of mind with respect to the problem of decoding lies is a curious one; when he comes close to raising it, instead of dealing with it, he will immediately turn his attention away from it. For example, in *De doctrina christiana*, we find the following comment: "Lying involves the will to speak falsely; thus we find many who wish to lie, but no one who wishes to be deceived." Instead of continuing immediately with an argument about how one might avoid being deceived, the text continues: "Since a man lies knowingly but suffers deception unwittingly, it is obvious that in a given instance a man who is deceived is better than a man who lies, because it is better to suffer iniquity that to perform it" (Book I, XXXVI [40], pp. 30–31). "Cum igitur hoc sciens homo faciat, illud nesciens patiatur, satis apparet in una eademque re illum, qui fallitur, eo qui mentitur esse meloirem, quando quidem pati melius est iniquitatem quam facere" (*De doctrina christiana*, Liber primus, XXXVI [40], p. 29).

8. M. J. Charlesworth, Introduction to *St. Anselm's Proslogion* (Notre Dame: University of Notre Dame Press, 1979), p. 43. The "question" which Charlesworth is considering concerns the relationship of faith to reason, and, as Charlesworth argues, that relationship for St. Anselm is much the same as the one which appears in St. Augustine. It is on matters of the nature and function of reason within that relationship where Anselm seems to have been an innovator. Although his contemporaries never questioned his orthodoxy, for some, "for Lanfranc [for example] it was St. Anselm's emphasis on 'reason' and his neglect of 'authorities' which represented a new, and perhaps dangerous, departure" (p. 43). It may be that Lanfranc's lack of enthusiasm for Anselm's methodology in arguing from reason stems from his own earlier conflict with Berengar of Tours, who, in his arguments against the possibility of a change of substance taking place in the Eucharist, had based his claim upon a grammatical rather than upon a scriptural premise. Berengar's argument "was briefly this: no proposition, consisting as it does of subject and predicate, can stand if the subject is denied, destroyed, or contradicted by the predicate. In particular no sentence with the subject *hic panis* or the equivalent pronoun *hoc* can stand if it proceeds to deny the substantial existence of the subject of the sentence: hence *Hic panis* (or *hoc*) *est corpus Christi* (or *meum*) would be self-contradictory if it implied that the substance of the subject of the sentence ceased to exist" (R. W. Southern, "Lanfranc of Bec and Berengar of Tours," in *Studies in Medieval History Presented to Frederick Maurice Powicke*, ed. R. W. Hunt, W. A. Pantin, and R. W. Southern [Oxford: At the Clarendon Press, 1948], p. 45). Anselm apparently learned from both Lanfranc and Berengar. From the difficulties encountered by the latter, he seems to have learned "that the right use of reason can never contradict Scripture. If Scripture clearly teaches a doctrine, then any rational argument to the contrary will be an unsound argument. [Its conclusion] becomes a signal cautioning one to take a second look at the alleged soundness of the proof or at the allegedly clear interpreta-

tion of Scripture" (Jasper Hopkins, *A Companion to the Study of St. Anselm* [Minneapolis: University of Minnesota Press, 1972], pp. 44–45). Everyone who writes on Anselm notices this: "In the *Monologion*, [Anselm] ambitiously undertakes to prove—by rational reflection alone, without recourse to the authority of Scripture—that God exists and is consistently triune" (Jasper Hopkins and Herbert Richardson, Translators' Preface to *Anselm of Canterbury*, vol. 1, 2nd ed. [Toronto: The Edwin Mellen Press, 1975], p. vii). The same kind of argument is made in the *Proslogion*. For Anselm, there is a conviction "that the spiritual requires the guidance of the rational just as the rational needs the vitality of the spiritual" (p. viii).

9. *De veritate*, in Hopkins and Richardson, *Anselm of Canterbury*, vol. 2 (Toronto: The Edwin Mellen Press, 1976), p. 86. The phrase provides the heading for chapter 7 of *De veritate*.

10. This is particularly evident in the transition from Book 5 of *De musica* to the beginning of Book 6. The first five books of *De musica* were probably begun in 387 A.D. prior to Augustine's baptism. Book 6 was probably written in 391. The first five books are a relatively traditional treatment of the art of meter and versification as it was taught in Augustine's time. Book 6 begins with a noticeable change: "We have delayed long enough and very childishly, too, through five books, in those number-traces belonging to time-intervals" (chapter 1 [1], p. 324, in *Writings of Saint Augustine*, vol. 2, in *The Fathers of the Church*, vol. 4 [New York: Fathers of the Church, Inc., 1947]). "Satis diu pene atque adeo plane pueriliter per quinque libros in vestigiis numerorum ad moras temporum pertinentium morati sumus" (*De musica*, Liber sextus, 1 [1], p. 486, in Aurelii Augustini, *De musica*, ed. Giovanni Marzi, Collana di Classici della Filosofia Cristiana, 1 [Florence: Sansoni, 1969]). The childish delay has resulted from Augustine's earlier inability to understand the divine, eternal nature of the "numbers" he has been dealing with, and it is that wisdom to which he turns his attention in Book 6: "Let us put our joy neither in carnal pleasure, nor in the honors and praises of men, nor in the exploring of things touching the body from without, having God within where all we love is sure and unchangeable" (*De mus.* 14 [48], p. 370). "Quamobrem neque in voluptate carnali, neque in honoribus et laudibus hominum, neque in eorum exploratione quae forinsecus corpus attingunt, nostra gaudia collocemus, habentes in intimo Deum, ubi certum est et incommutabile omne quod amamus" (*De mus.* 14 [48], p. 618). It is the eternal, abstract, and mathematical in rhythm, not the sensual pleasure of rhythmic sounds, that should engage us. The import of this sixth book is reemphasized later in Augustine's *Retractations:* "The sixth of these [six books "On Music"] became especially well known because in it a subject worthy of investigation was considered, namely, how, from corporeal and spiritual but changeable numbers, one comes to the knowledge of unchangeable numbers which are already in unchangeable truth itself" (Saint Augustine, *The Retractations*, 10 [1], p. 45, in *The Fathers of the Church*, vol. 60 [Washington D. C.: The Catholic University of America Press, 1968]). "Quorum ipse sextus maxime innotuit, quoniam res in eo cognitione digna uersatur, quomodo a corporalibus et spiritalibus, sed mutabilibus numeris preueniatur ad immutabiles numeros, qui iam in ipsa sunt immutabili ueritate" (Sancti Aureli Augustini, *Retractationum*, ed. Pius Knoll, in *Corpus scriptorum ecclesiasticorum latinorum*, vol. 36 [Sancti Aureli Augustini, *Opera*, sect. I, pars 2] [Vienna: F. Tempsky, 1902], X [1], p. 52). The emphasis is upon how one gets *from* the corporeal and changeable *to* the unchangeable.

11. Anselm sensed in his own work little difference from Augustine. "As he himself repeatedly said, his only ambition was to restate what his master Augustine

has already stated" (Etienne Gilson, *Reason and Revelation in the Middle Ages* [New York: Charles Scribner's Sons, 1938], pp. 23–24). Augustine, however, was by training a rhetorician who came to Christianity from the study of Platonic and Neoplatonic writings. Anselm's circumstances were different. In his time, "the standard science was Logic. Under such circumstances, the [endeavor to understand the nature of the Christian faith] was bound to result in a new translation of Christian beliefs into terms of logical demonstration" (Gilson, p. 25). The logic which Anselm's generation inherited comes largely from Boethius's readings of Aristotle, and it did not come into Anselm's hands ready to answer the kinds of questions that were being asked by the thinkers of his time. Anselm was by training a grammarian and was particulary sensitive to the kinds of questions which linguistic usage raised. More centrally for him than for Augustine, the nature of human language and the kinds of truth it could embody were sensitive issues to be examined and defined as precisely as possible. Although Anselm would never err as Berengar had done and try to read the grammatical categories of human grammar back directly upon Scripture, he seems to have been one of the first of a long series of medieval thinkers who wished to extend to its limit what we might now call the "truth value" of human language.

12. Saint Anselm, *Philosophical Fragments*, in *Anselm of Canterbury*, vol. 2, p. 6. "Omne de quo aliquod verbum dicitur, aliqua causa est ut sit hoc quod verbo illo significatur" ("The Anselmian Miscellany in Lambeth MS. 59," p. 343, in *Memorials of St. Anselm*, ed. R. W. Southern and F. S. Schmitt [London: The British Academy, Oxford University Press, 1969], pp. 333–54). As anyone who has looked into medieval grammar knows, the verb *signify* is problematical. For Anselm, there is "an intrinsic, natural truth in speech, a *veritas enuntiationis*, in virtue of the fact that a statement signifies truly what its speaker means. This natural significative function pertains to all of their speakers, they are accidentally true. It is this latter type of truth that Anselm dignifies with the name rectitude'" (Marcia L. Colish, *The Mirror of Language: A Study in the Medieval Theory of Knowledge* [New Haven: Yale University Press, 1968], pp. 112–13). See also Desmond Paul Henry, *The Logic of St. Anselm* (Oxford: At the Clarendon Press, 1967), especially chapter 8, "Truth and Ethics," pp. 230–39. There are two more recent essays by Marcia L. Colish which examine this same issue: "The Stoic Theory of Verbal Signification" and "St. Anselm's Philosophy of Language Reconsidered," in *Anselm Studies*, ed. Gillian R. Evans, 1982 [forthcoming]).

13. "Quidquid autem facere dicitur, aut facit ut sit aliquid, aut facit ut non sit aliquid. Omne igitur 'facere' dici potest aut facere esse aut facere non esse, quae duo sunt affirmationes contrariae. Quarum negationes sunt: 'non facere esse,' et 'non facere non esse.' Sed affirmatio 'facere esse' ponitur aliquando pro negatione, quae est 'non facere non esse'; et conversim 'non facere non esse' pro 'facere esse.' Similiter 'facere non esse' et 'non facere esse' pro invicem ponuntur" ("The Anselmian Miscellany in Lambeth MS.59" pp. 343–44).

14. The diagram is reproduced from *Anselm of Canterbury*, vol. 2, p. 36. The nature of Anselm's logic has been analyzed most thoroughly and most often by Desmond Paul Henry. There are extended symbolic examinations both in his edition of *The De Grammatico of St. Anselm* (Notre Dame: University of Notre Dame Press, 1964), pp. 103–64, and in *The Logic of Saint Anselm* (Oxford: At the Clarendon Press, 1967). These examinations have indicated that, although there is a great variety in the kinds of problems Anselm chooses to tackle, "there exists a striking contrast between the variety which they display and the systematic unity of the

method whereby he does tackle them. . . . Anselm's solutions . . . are not *ad hoc,* and are not at all lacking in interrelation" (*The Logic of Saint Anselm,* p. 119). Looking more widely, not only at Anselm but at his followers as well, Henry discovers much methodological consonance with Anselm among Ockham, Abelard, and other later thinkers concerned immediately with problems resulting from the interrelation of language and truth (*Medieval Logic and Metaphysics: A Modern Introduction* [London: Hutchinson University Library, 1972]).

15. *Anselm of Canterbury,* vol. 2, p. 87. "Sed secundum rei veritatem quomodo possumus dicere, quia quidquid est debet esse, cum sint multa opera mala, quae certum est esse non debere?" (*De ver.,* Capitulum VIII, p. 186, in S. Anselmi Cantuariensis Archiepiscopi, *Opera omnia,* vol. 1, ed. F. S. Schmitt [Stuttgart: Friedrich Frommann, 1968], pp. 169–99).

16. "Idem igitur debet esse et non esse. Debet enim esse, quia bene et sapienter ab eo, quo non permittente fieri non posset permittitur; et non debet esse quantum ad illum cuius iniqua voluntate concipitur. Hoc igitur modo dominus IESUS, quia solus innocens erat, non debuit mortem pati, nec ullus eam illi debuit inferre; et tamen debuit eam pati, quia ipse sapienter et benigne et utiliter voluit eam sufferre. Multis enim modis eadem res suscipit diversis considerationibus contraria" (*De ver.,* VIII, pp. 86–87).

17. Anselm's direct influence declined rapidly after the eleventh century as the disposition and apparent neglect of the manuscripts of his texts indicate (see Colish, *The Mirror of Language,* pp. 156–60). His influence upon the later Middle Ages is, then, quite different from Augustine's. Augustine's works and his thought were never very distant from any center of intellectual activity from his own time until beyond the fourteenth century. He remained a source for medieval thinking about the relation of faith to reason. Anselm is not such a source; he is, instead, a symptom, the first clear instance of the emergence of logic as the instrument of reason in the pursuit of the understanding of faith. The causes of Anselm's decline remain a puzzle. It is true that the questions he asks and the methods he uses to answer them are not unlike those asked and employed by the thinkers of the twelfth and thirteenth centuries. Why then was Anselm not a more frequently employed model for disputation? It is possible that at least one reason for his declining influence can be found in the way in which questions came, after Anselm's time, to be asked. Anselm was a quietly orthodox man in matters of belief. "Left to himself he was a thinker remarkably free from doubts and uncertainties" (Gillian R. Evans, *Anselm and a New Generation* [Oxford: Clarendon Press, 1980], p. 8). Reason, as he employed it, raised no theological problems for him. However, for Anselm's successors, matters of theology became "open" questions. When Anselm "says that men should use their reason to help them understand their faith[,] he intends them to do so only in order to understand what they ought already to believe, and not to seek out new items of faith so as to extend the range of their beliefs. His successors could not, however, expect to go back to first principles and find them undisturbed" (ibid., p. 9). It is in their doubts that he casts his shadow over the whole scholastic movement of the thirteenth and fourteenth centuries.

18. Carleton Brown, ed., *Religious Lyrics of the XVth Century* (Oxford: The Clarendon Press, 1939), p. 120. The paradoxical idea which the poem embodies is not a new one. It "had from an early date formed part of the Easter liturgy[,] but it seems to have passed from there into poetry only in the later Middle Ages" (Rosemary Woolf, *The English Religious Lyric in the Middle Ages* [Oxford: At the Clarendon Press, 1968], p. 290). This poem accompanies another well-known paradox poem,

"The Maiden Makeles," in BM MS Sloane 2593. This poem too develops as a central theme an apparent contradiction, this time the one which inheres in the linguistic opposition of maiden to mother. This kind of semantic play is not uncommon in medieval lyrics generally. There is evidence to suggest that the poem "The Maiden Makeles," as we have it, had been worked and reworked and its central paradox strengthened over about two hundred years (Stephen Manning, "I syng of a myden," *PMLA*, 75 (1960), 8–12).

19. "Ex animi enim sui sententia, non ex rerum ipsarum ueritate uel falsitate mentiens aut non mentiens iudicandus est" (*De men.*, III [3], p. 415).

20. This "true speech" is usually referred to as *myrie* "merry" speech in Middle English, but the term is not our term *merry*. In *The Canterbury Tales,* for example, the tales which are directly referred to as "myrie" are the prose tale of Melibee (Group B², 2154) and the *Parson's Tale* (Group I, 46). The Host, Harry Bailly, asks the Clerk twice to tell a *myrie* tale (Group E, 9, 15). He also asks the Pardoner for one (Group C, 316–19), and the Pardoner agrees to do so. Whether or not the Pardoner's tale is "myrie" is a problem addressed here later. For Chaucer and for his contemporaries, *myrie* regularly referred not only to situations which are "pleasant," as our contemporary usage denotes, but to speech acts in which positive intent is matched directly with positive speech. It is instructional, doctrinal, and useful. It moves as close as any speech of man can toward the nature of Scripture. We must, however, keep in mind that "myrie" speech is human speech; Scripture is something else altogether. See Lois Ebin, "Chaucer, Lydgate, and the myrie' Tale," *Chaucer Review*, 13 (1979), 316–36.

21. If not of his *modus vivendi*. It depends, of course, on the degree to which the Pardoner is or is not in control of his own will. If, to take the less likely option, the Pardoner directly and fully believes *everything* he says, he is a jangler and a teller of "falsehoods" in Augustine's sense. His speech should then produce an effect rather like that produced by the Wife of Bath as she speaks. Under such circumstances, he would be just plain lucky to get anyone to believe anything he says. No one, to my knowledge, interprets the Pardoner this way. He is doing something else.

22. All quotations from Chaucer are from F. N. Robinson, ed., *The Works of Geoffrey Chaucer*, 2nd ed. (Boston: Houghton Mifflin, 1957). *The Canterbury Tales* are referred to by the group letters and line numbers in this edition.

23. "Unde etiam duplex cor dicitur esse mentientis, id est duplex cogitatio: una rei eius, quam ueram esse uel scit uel putat et non profert; altera eius rei, quam pro ista profert sciens falsam esse uel putans" (*De men.*, III [3], p. 415).

24. It is one of those kinds of speech which Augustine identified in *De magistro* as not expressing what is in the mind of the speaker. It occurs when "speech, frequently repeated and memorized, flows out of the speaker's mouth while he is thinking of something else, as often happens to us when we are singing a hymn" (13 [42], pp. 56–57). "Sermo memoriae mandatus et saepe decursus alia cogitantis ore funditur, quod nobis cum hymnum canimus saepe contingit" (XIII [42], p. 51). The Pardoner has his mind here on the rhetorical polish of what is coming out of his mouth. In this his procedure is in contradistinction to that of St. Augustine himself, who, in writing the *De mendacio*, abandoned his rhetoric to the necessities of immediate expression: "Do not look [in the *De mendacio*] for striking phraseology. In my endeavor to probe into the various points involved and to put into form as quickly as possible a work of such tremendous import for the regulation of daily living, I have paid scant, and, indeed, almost negligible attention to the selection of words" (*De men.*, 1, p. 54). "Eloquim noli quaerere; multum enim de rebus laborau-

imus et de celeritate absoluendi tam necessarii cotidianae uitae operis: unde tenuis, as prope nulla fuit nobis cura uerborum" (De men., I [1], p. 414). The very particular care with which the Pardoner invests his speech has been seen by some as a reflection of the excesses practiced by the rhetoricians of the second sophistic of late classical times. These orators and writers about oratory favored effectiveness of delivery over soundness of argument. Excessive gesture, widely modulated voice in delivery, and theatricality were its hallmarks. "If such theatrical delivery seems to moderns of the West more violent than it seemed to its own audiences, it has never been extinct; and any one familiar with the oratory of display in any time will recognize the sophist's heavy frown, his mein of deep thought, his air of authority. Chaucer's Pardoner speaks for the whole sophist line" (Charles Sears Baldwin, Medieval Rhetoric and Poetic (to adj) Interpreted from Representative Works) [New York: Macmillan, 1928], p. 16). Although the features of delivery are there, the Pardoner is much too concerned with the argument he is presenting to provide a good example of a typical sophistical orator.

25. "Exceptis igitur iocis, quae numquam sunt putata mendacia—habent enim euidentissimam ex pronuntiatione atque ipso iocantis affectu significationem animi nequaquam fallentis" (De men. II [2], p. 414). The MED (Part J.1, pp. 372–75) gives as the most common reference of jape (n.) "trick," "deceit," or "fraud." To tell japes is to engage in "frivolous pastimes" or "literary trifles." To jape (v.) is to "deceive," or "trick," or to "behave foolishly." Most of these are contexts of minor immediate import. When something of greater significance is to be referred to, a pejorative adjective is used: angri jape, fel jape. The word is probably derived from OF japer "howl," "chatter," "gossip," hence our words yap and gab. Such an etymology places verbal japes in a position of near synonymy with jangling, where, logically, they ought to be.

26. The term is the one used, finally, by Donald Howard to account for the peculiar attraction of the Pardoner himself: "He is a mystery, an enigma" (The Idea of the Canterbury Tales [Berkeley and Los Angeles: University of California Press, 1976], p. 345). My concern here is not with the character of Pardoner (he surely embodies all the enigmatic and problematical characteristics Howard finds in him) but with the peculiar ending to his tale telling. Howard considers the ending, too: "There is no way of telling whether his attempted joke or trick at the end is an afterthought" (p. 363). Howard offers a good review of many of the explanations which have been offered for what is going on. None is fully convincing. Each makes sense, but leaves us feeling unsettled. Because the text makes no explanation, any explanation we offer we impose upon it, and it is at every turn prepared to dodge us.

27. Silence is interesting in its own right. It is as variable as speech. If we map it back upon the four-cornered logical model which was useful in diagramming varieties of speech, above, we will find that we can have a "true" silence of spiritual meditation (A) corresponding to true, "merry" speech. Contrary to that is the lie of silence (B). In both the De mendacio and Contra mendacium, particularly chapters 11, 13, and 16 of the former and chapters 10 and 18 of the latter, Augustine exemplifies as lying the refusal to speak in contexts which require true speech (see Marcia L. Colish, "St. Augustine's Rhetoric of Silence Revisited," Augustinian Studies, 9 [1978], 15–24). On "true" silence, see Joseph Anthony Mazzeo, "St. Augustine's Rhetoric of Silence," Journal of the History of Ideas, 23 (1962), 175–96. What we can now add are the other two logical silences. Contradictory to "true" silence and consentient with lying silence would occur (C), what we must call a "jangling" silence, a silence inappropriate to its context or imperfectly realized

somehow. The best example we have of this is the bungled silence resulting from Parzival's not asking the appropriate question of the Fisher King. There ought to be, then, contrary to this "jangling" silence, a nonjangling and appropriate silence discreetly inappropriate to the contexts of jangling and lying, and consentient with "true" silence. It is, of course, the silent equivalent of the beneficent lie. It ought to be created, if things had worked out as they had been earlier arranged, by the conclusion of Pardoner's tale telling. That we get a sullen void instead of this is at one with the result of the Pardoner's speech as well. Chaucer seems to have been much interested in examining silence in just this way; the possible uses of "discretionary silence" form one of the major focuses of the *Manciple's Tale*, Group H of *The Canterbury Tales*, especially from about line 309 to the end (362).

28. "Aut ergo cauenda mendacia recte agendo aut confitenda sunt paenitendo; non autem, cum abundent infeliciter uiuendo, augenda sunt et docendo" (*Contra men.* XXI [41], pp. 526–27).

Penance, Irony, and Chaucer's Retraction

Robert S. Knapp

Chaucer's Retraction—pious, conventional, and no doubt unironic in its dominant meaning—sets up a multiple problem in the relationship between game and earnest.[1] Most immediately, the Retraction complicates our attitudes toward the preceding *Canterbury Tales*, compelling us to worry about how these mostly playful texts square with the sober and unconcealed intentions of a pilgrim who has finally fixed his eyes upon the celestial Jerusalem. But we cannot address this problem without opening up the still more essentially contested question of the relationship between any text and the supposed intentions of its author, whenever and however stated. By an easy extension, this further question can also be seen as a problem about game and earnest: it concerns the separation of ironical chaff from fruitful sincerity, or of reader's play and rereader's judgment from writer's sentence and design.

Though theoretical considerations may make us doubt that sharp boundaries mark off one of these domains from its contrary, we nonetheless have to keep sorting for the difference between them. Thinking itself depends upon such separations, as does speech; without them, there would not be even a provisional distinction between making sense and making noise.[2] Yet game and earnest, like every such pair of contrasting terms, acquire meaning only in relation to each other. For this reason, it is hard to imagine a clear and distinct sobriety fully insulated from playfulness, or to conceive of something playful which has no use or meaning. It is just as hard to imagine a set of words utterly purified of historical intentions and representational power, or to think of meaning something without embodying it in text, which being semiotic,

45

must also be inherently playful and potentially misleading.[3] Nonetheless, by so completely renouncing wordly works, Chaucer seems to effect this very divorce between flesh and spirit. Just before disappearing from mortal view, he absents himself from his poems, abolishes his authority in them, and leaves us this troublesome division between a few fruitful tracts and a great body of chaff now condemned for being what we moderns—and his Parson, though in a different moral tone of voice—would call the purely "textual."[4]

One way to think about so perplexing a result is to describe the Retraction as a gradual process of authorial self-elimination. "Heere taketh the mekere of this book his leve," says the rubric, and just so we don't forget which book it is that he's leaving and we're being left with, the Retraction goes on to enumerate all those translations and "enditynges of worldly vanities" that Chaucer wants to disown. Mere worldlings might think that such a confession of fault is really a way of establishing a canon and proclaiming one's fame, but Chaucer no sooner permits these effects than he goes on to leave them and his writer's ego behind: all he claims for his own as he steps into an order of reality where earnest never mixes with game are his translations of Boethius and other unnamed "bookes of legendes of seintes, and omelies, and moralitee, and devocioun."[5] Which is to say that all he will admit of his own voice is its vehicular service in making better voices heard. But even these other voices are deprived of personal identity. Not only are they mostly anonymous, but as we infer from earlier reference to that "litel tretys" which must be the *Parson's Tale* and which is surely all translation and redaction, if there is anything in these secondhand texts which pleases the reader, for that thank "oure lord Jhesu Crist, of whom procedeth al wit and al goodnesse." If anything displeases, however, ascribe that to lack of skill "and nat to my wyl that wolde ful fayn have seyd bettre if I hadde had konnynge." In short, "'Al that is writen is writen for oure doctrine,' and that is myn entente."[6] Thus joined in intention with the saving Word and with a set of other men's texts presumably manifesting the same intention, a now thoroughly effaced "Chaucer" prays for grace to do a proper penance, and promptly vanishes into a Latin credal formula, "Qui cum patre etc."

Though the foregoing description differs in emphasis from other modern attempts to understand the effect of Chaucer's Retraction, it shares in their widespread consensus. For most critics, the Retraction marks Chaucer's movement from one order of reality to another: from an order where irony and fiction have their place to an order beyond the limitations—and hence beyond the ironies—both of mortality and of art. Not everyone admires this movement: some see it as regrettable capitulation to orthodoxy, others as limited by its very conventionality to local rather than global effects within the *Canterbury Tales*. But few see irony in the Retraction itself.[7] If Chaucer's palinode generates any ironies at all, they seem to be those that Alfred David remarks upon, ones which cause us to doubt the reality of the world in which we have been immersed. "The conclusion of the *Canterbury Tales* is like an awakening."[8]

Of course one can awaken in different ways. Patristic critics would have the Retraction awaken us to a rereading of the ostensibly abandoned tales, a rereading that works everything into a charitable harmony manifesting fruit rather than chaff. Others would leave the tales more or less as they seem, having us awaken not to hidden (and problematic) sentence, but to the absolute difference between fallible art and infallible religious truth: Chaucer does not really wish us to ignore his secular games, just to put them in perspective, to see them for the chaff that they must be by comparison with earnest eternity. In a later stage of my argument, I will urge that this disagreement among critics—which responds to a certain ambivalence within the *Canterbury Tales*—reflects the imperfect distinction which E.D. Hirsch has tried to draw between meaning and significance.[9] But for now it is enough that almost everyone agrees that the Retraction establishes—or tries to establish—an absolute difference between the impure world of veils and riddles and the pure world of ultimate, unveiled truth.

My account deviates from this view by calling attention to the logic of cancellation and withdrawal. To describe the Retraction as an act of authorial self-abnegation really implies that this last Chaucerian gesture bears a curious formal likeness to the ironies and artifice it ostensibly eschews. Not that Chaucer does not mean what he says: he plainly intends nothing which conflicts with God's intention to instruct us toward salvation, and he wants now to "doon in this present lyf . . . so that I may been oon of hem at the day of doome that shulle be saved." Chaucer evidently wants to efface the distance between his will and God's, jettisoning everything that might compromise his conformity with Christ. But in so sincerely separating his final intentions and the words of orthodoxy from the bulk of his previous works, while apparently making no effort to deny us access to those works, Chaucer—as usual—puts the burden of judgment on his readers. We must decide for ourselves—apart from the author's final understanding and intentions—which tales "sownen into synne."

Casting up the curtain on eschatological hopes while provocatively veiling the flesh he leaves behind, Chaucer's Retraction thus looks like the last movement in a prolonged concatenation of local ironies. This affinity between the prescinding retraction and distancing irony grows less latent when we consider that a palinode, by taking back what has just been said, attempts at the last moment to lay hold on just that freedom from adverse judgement which irony tries to dwell within continuously. We might even say that this palinode does fully what Geoffrey's lesser ironies only do in part. Abolishing its author's worldly ego, the Retraction leaves the readers with nothing but an empty carapace of "Chaucerian" texts, all ironized as error beside the living Word and the good doctrine of His acknowledged servants, from whose voice the real (and fully absent) Chaucer—now truly a simple and right-minded pilgrim—hopes his "own" will be indistinguishable.[10] One fleeting advantage of this approach is that it goes beyond appeals to the alterity of medieval piety and literature to propose a purely formal reason why the Retraction cannot be ironic with respect to its principal declared intentions: palinodes and ironies perform similar negative gestures. Both procedures try to institute a wholly transcendent, spiritual, and "saved" ego; both express a finite being's determination to mean nothing which can be tripped up by a better and perhaps last and infinitely penetrating judgment; both try to effect a text which will be forever invulnerable, a text in which no particular, fallible, and temporal intender can be run to ground and punished for that very fault. Yet such parallels, however suggestive they may be, hardly prove a strict equivalence between irony and retraction. Quite the contrary. Even ignoring the fact that retraction follows a text whereas irony seems to happen inside one, no formal analogy can long obscure the more basic truth that Chaucer's Retraction is a religious act of penance, which ought therefore to stand opposed to literary irony precisely as earnest does to game. Far from reconciling penitential sentence with literary play, the discovery of even a partial affinity between irony and retraction all the more starkly defines their apparent semantic contrast.

All the same, one senses some prospect of an interesting paradox, brought about by overlap between playful and serious strategies of detachment. What brings the paradox into focus is just the fact that despite the way in which irony and retraction share a certain logic of self-abnegation, it seems to violate common sense and underlying metaphor to collapse penance into the same fundamental trope. After all, irony by etymology has to do with masquerade, whereas penance is associated with punishment. Indeed, insofar as the ironist trades in riddles, fictions, and half-truths, he would seem as much to merit punishment as St. Paul's "old man," whose deceit, tale-telling, and theatrical fraud is just what a penitent Christian wants to chastise himself for and cast off. Irony is evasive and riddling, often amoral, and never quite sincere; even when practiced with moral intentions, it is always—like all verbal tropes—indirect and (self-)protective. Penance is just the reverse, a movement of self-denial in moral and therefore in tropological substance as well as in form, a gesture which means to abolish the false and reveal the true, even if revelation requires the reenactment of Christ's physical sorrows as well as the spiritual imitation of his service. Jests and scandalous riddles; plain speech and a holy life: the turn of signifiers and the turn toward Jerusalem seem unalterably opposed.

Yet both are tropes nevertheless, turning away from finite error toward infinite freedom. The difference is just that penance, by dealing with the embodied spirit rather than the mask of words, claims in effect to be more intensely devoted to the letter than literature can ever be. Where irony saves mere words (and their speaker's liberty) by sacrificing a false double, penance would save the flesh itself (and the soul which is its form) by much the same strategy, punishing and casting away a false old man in order to renew the whole Body of mankind and join it to the Word. In exchanging literature for religion, then, Chaucer merely gives up a weak semiotic system in favor of a stronger one.

But what if that stronger semiotic system were subject (except for grace) to the same fluidity and partial indeterminancy as language itself? If penance redoubles irony in form, perhaps it does so in other respects as well, for the flesh is no less indeterminate—no less dependent upon its "hearer's" construction—than any other vehicle of signification. In pursuit of this possibility, I want to work out more details of the suggestion that penance and irony, by operating in similar ways at different semiotic levels, have a genuine albeit paradoxical affinity.

Since penance has at least the advantage over irony of being reasonably well defined, I want to begin by rehearsing some of that definition.[11] Penance, of course, is a sacrament; like the six others, it therefore partakes of semiotics, morality, and theology all at once. In the standard formula of Isidore of Seville, "A sacrament is any celebration in which the activity is done in such a way as to signify something which is taken for sacred; . . . under cover of the corporal act, the divine power secretly works our salvation."[12] That is to say, a sacrament is an outward sign (sacramentum tantum) of an inward and hidden effect (res) of which it is (as sacramentum et res) the cause, both instrumental and formal: sacraments secretly "effect what they figuratively express."[13] In more expansive terms, the outward sign or sacramentum tantum is a figurative expression of an inward grace which it secretly causes; this grace, present in the living soul and its activity, is both sign and reality (sacramentum et res,) and in turn causes the final effect of salvation, which being wholly real is called res tantum. In short, a sacrament is a sanctifying sign which produces an inner moral transformation that itself becomes both a sign and a further real cause of the signified reality that is salvation.

The suitably Chaucerian example of pilgrimage ought to give substance to this definition. As all readers of Augustine know, pilgrimage is a penitential activity and state of being which signifies a certain attitude toward signs. The pilgrim is a Christian who knows that the things and deeds of this world are not ends in themselves (res tantum) but corporal and temporal visibilia (res et signa) which though not sacramental nonetheless point to the eternal and spiritual things of God. Homo viator, therefore, must comport himself toward creation as if everything were a vehicle and nothing but God the resting place on his journey: he must treat the world as if it were fiction, to be read actively for sense and not passively for self-indulgence and escape. In other words, the pilgrim must avoid treating as an idol the text through which he travels. As a good reader, which is to say a penitential one, he knows that this world means more than it seems, knows too that his own attempts to construe the world are subject to error. For this reason, there is in his behavior a continuous self-denial: as he holds himself back from the world (for to enjoy the world is to treat it as signified rather than signifier), so he also withholds full assent from his own exegesis (for what seems to be fruit may turn out to be chaff). He realizes that whatever construction he places on the world will be wrong insofar as it is partial; that whatever advice he gives to others must, as the Parson says, be subject to "correccioun / Of clerkes, for I am nat textueel" (56–57). To read the world in this way of habitual penance is, then, just to stay on that old, "righte wey of Jerusalem celestial" (79–80).

In this description of penance, I have adopted the modern habit of treating the world as a text and ourselves as its readers, a habit with evident affinities to well-known medieval views of a world made by the Word and still carrying traces and reflections of that divine Author. Yet our only authority for Chaucer's views on penance—the Parson himself—says little about reading or misreading. His favorite tropes are so commonplace that they hardly seem figurative at all: sin is error, wandering from the way; or else it is foulness, ingratitude, loss, and disorder. To be sure, he initially—and rather suggestively, for my purposes— identifies old paths with old sentences that are to be interrogated for information about the right way to travel in order to know God and attain bliss. But he quickly drops this hint of a lexical metaphor in order to lay out the varieties and remedies of sin according to the familiar figure of the tree and its branches.[14] Subsequently he departs even from that figure, ultimately achieving in relatively spare and unmetaphorical language an expository lucidity unparalleled in other penitential manuals.[15] Though the Parson refers to Augustine, he quotes just slogans and tags, saying nothing about either the Augustinian doctrine of signs or about the sacramental character of penance. One might therefore conclude that sacramental semiotics are irrelevant to Chaucer, that the metaphor of reading is just a modern heuristic, and that the connections I seek between penance and contemporary literary theory are simply factitious.

Subsequent discussion should show that these connections would be useful even if they lacked deeper grounding in medieval thought and practice. Indeed, the kinship that I seek to show between penance and irony can come clear only when medieval penitential theory receives some translation into modern categories: I do not suppose that Chaucer was fully aware of that kinship, nor that his audience would have accepted a formulation such as the one that I propose. Thus lexical metaphors, though evidently rooted in a long-standing and specifically Christian fascination with the world as book, must be understood in the first instance as modern ways of shedding light on largely foreign and forgotten practices. Yet the metaphor of reading fits both penance and Chaucer's work with particular ease. The general theory of sacraments and the specific theory of penance require a doctrine of signs and sign-making and imply a lexical view of reality. Chaucer's poetry becomes increasingly focused on the interaction between teller, tale, audience, and the larger—still semiotic—context: an evidently lexical interaction.[16] And since his Parson's understanding of penance is highly orthodox, relying upon notions that would be unintelligible without an assumed knowledge of Christian semiotics, I do not think that the silence of this "litel tretys" about a specific figure of "reading" should cause concern.

Indeed, had Chaucer made much of this figure in the *Parson's Tale,* the crucial—if problematic—distinction between taletelling (imaginative literature) and truth-telling (religious counsel) would lose some force: it is essential to the tension between the *Parson's Tale* and the others that it block some of the figurative and lexical implications of penitential doctrine. One senses here the sort of dialectic between blindness and insight of which Paul de Man has informed us, a dialectic which depends upon the oscillation between modes of utterance, one a matter of metaphoric substitution, the other a matter of synecdochic or metonymic association and connection.[17] Until more of the workings of penance have been laid out, however, it will have to remain an open question whether or not such a dialectic is at work between penance and irony.

It is no open question, however, that medieval penitential theory—especially the theory of the early and influential *Summa* by Raymond of Penaforte, which is one of Chaucer's principal sources—gives special emphasis to the individual Christian's will in the process of sign-making and spiritual transformation.[18] Since later theory gives more weight to priestly absolution, it might seem particularly emphatic in a fourteenth-century context for a parson to stress—as this one does—the active character of penance. Such a central place for the will in the task of reforming one's soul to its original image and likeness means in turn that penance is a special sacrament. It shares with marriage this ethical and performative uniqueness: the individual's own acts, rather than some substance which the priest handles, make up the corporal matter which is the sign of the effect that the sacrament causes. These acts constitute the efficacious figure of salvation; they are (with grace) sufficient for that effect (though the priest's words are normally the necessary formal complement to the matter of these acts).[19]

But penance differs even from marriage in that these sacramental acts are self-reflexive: as St. Augustine puts it, "Penitence is a kind of vengeance of the one sorrowing, always punishing in himself that which he deplores having committed."[20] This is the true metanoia, a turn (or trope) of the soul against the soul, of the sinner's will against his will. Penance cancels false movement; it is a self-directed negativity, turning from vanity toward that self-sacrificing God of whom the penitent is thus not only the created but also the active sign, no longer a "sone of ire" but now a "sone of grace" (312).[21] Because of this unique emphasis on acts of the will directed against other acts of the will, penance has an acutely paradoxical nature: the deeds of a finite and fallen creature come through divine acceptance to signify an infinite forgiveness. At its uttermost, in the life of habitual penance, the struggle against sin becomes not a sign of the Fall, but of conformity with the whole Body of Christ, a perpetual reenactment and completion of the atoning sacrifice that freed humanity from sin and its punishment. The trope of penance, then, is both metaphor and synecdoche, both a likeness and a part of which stands for the whole: by this negative and self-reflexive figure, the penitent both restores the divine Image in his soul and rejoins the communion of saints which is Christ's Body.[22]

The terms of this description should not only help confirm the argument that penance has a structural affinity to irony, but should also suggest that penance can be usefully analyzed as having both a cognitive and a performative dimension.[23] From the cognitive side, penance is a propositional sign—God's to us and ours to Him and each other—which purports to convey some truth about the divine essence and the human particulars which mirror it, for instance, that God intends our salvation, that some sinner is heartily sorry for his unlikeness to Christ and means to reconform himself to the will of God, or as in the case of St. Francis or *los penitentes* of the American Southwest, that Christ was something like this person, stigmata and all. From the performative side, penance is a causal and persuasive activity: the divine activity of giving grace and accepting satisfaction and the human activity of repenting, confessing, and making such amends as alms-giving, self-flagellation, or going on pilgrimage. Put this way, one might expect to find just the same relation between these analytic dimensions of penance as between any other performative-cognitive pair, say between intending something and the texts which our intentions produce.[24] I think that this is the case, but the problem is complicated in an interesting way by the fact that in penance there is obviously a double performative origin and a double cognitive referent, for penance is performed by the activity of both God and man and also refers to both God and man. To put it another way, in penance the relation between speaker and hearer is not so straightforward as it seems to be in ordinary speech, for God and the individual each stand at each moment on both sides of that divide.[25]

This doubleness is necessary to prevent what would otherwise be a debilitating failure of knowledge and power at each of the conventional three stages of penance: contrition of heart, confession of mouth, and satisfaction of deed. Were it not for the cooperation of God and man, there would be at each stage an insurmountable difficulty in equating text and intention, which stand in relation one to the other as finite to infinite when the text is man's (whether taken as performative or constative) and the saving intention God's, or as infinite to finite when the text is God himself, as the Word, and the intention is man's.

To see how this difficulty comes into being and is resolved, it is necessary to dwell a moment on the cognitive and performative aspects of each part of the total movement of penance.

Contrition, says the Parson, "is the verray sorwe that a man receyveth in his herte for his synnes, with sad purpos to shryve him, and to do penance and nevermoore to do synne" (128). As my account so far should suggest, one can usefully understand sin as semiotic and moral deformation.[26] Originally created in the image and likeness of God and restored to that image through baptism (the first plank after shipwreck, in Jerome's famous metaphor), the sinner warps himself away from his exemplar and original by un-Christlike behavior (behavior which is often called "unkynd," in a suggestive play between the senses of kind as "essence" or "nature" and kind as "compassionate").[27] It would seem that contrition must always be inadequate, if not impossible, by reason of the incapacity of finite human beings to know and love an infinite God, and thus to be adequately sorry for their difference from Him and their ingratitude for His sacrifice.[28] The confirmation of this supposition is the fact of venial sin, our endemic slowness to love, which vitiates human capacities to know and do good. (The Parson addresses venial sin in lines 357–85.) But in practice, the grace of the revealed law, old and new, is in itself enough to convict us of sin, and to inspire in us a reformative fear and love, that "continuell" contrition which the Parson recommends (304), together with that "brennynge love ... to oure lord Jesu Crist" which can "restreyne" us from venial sin.[29] We need not comprehend the whole text of that Trinity which we signify in order to know, and regret, that we have misread and misapplied the letter of ourselves and of the world.

Where contrition—that "roote . . . that hideth hym in the herte of him that is verray repentaunt" (111)—is a movement of the will dependent on a new spirit that recognizes previous misreadings of oneself, the world, and therefore of God, confession is the speech-act that is "signe of contricioun" (316). The limitation on confession is the familiar and devastating one of saying the truth, the whole truth, and nothing but the truth. Here it is not enough to passively recognize a wrong reading. For a perfect confession, "al moot be seyd, and no thyng excused ne hid ne forwrapped; and noght avaunte thee of thy goode werkes" (319). Unhappily, we do not know as we are known, for our sins—"as seith Seint Augustyn" (380)—are without number; it is therefore impossible to confess them adequately. At the least, one always risks saying too little (out of ignorance and pride) or saying too much (out of false humility). In the first case, the sin is obvious; in the second, "though thow ne were nat in synne biforn, yet artow thanne in synne thurgh thy lesynges" (1019). In practice, of course, the intention to make a perfect confession suffices, but that is only through the grace of God and the gift of his Son who as both Logos and Truth itself was the only perfect match between signifier and signified that we have ever known.

With satisfaction, there is still greater potential for error. Here the penitent is not simply describing all the ways of his previous misreading and misbehaving. Satisfaction amounts to restoring the text, to making amends, to writing anew: it is the fruit by which the root of contrition becomes known (115). But restoration is impossible—whether in literature or in life—unless some supplement again makes up the difference. The grossness of the body, the cloud of sin, what we might aptly call the play of *différance* that keeps us away from whatever might be behind the trace of writing, all this inevitably vitiates every attempt, however well intentioned, of restoring Eden or singing the new song. All that can bridge this gap is the sacrifice itself, the only perfect satisfaction, God's having placed his own Word and self *sous râture*. For that is one modern way to understand the Crucifixion: it is God, crossed; written and canceled at the same time. To the extent that human penance is modeled on this original sacrifice, the same logic operates in it, except in an inverse fashion. Where God, in the visible *figura* of the Son, speaks a perfect Word which is veiled, removed, taken back in the moment of fullest revelation, humankind must in deeds and words speak imperfectly, seeking through self-cancellation to erase those differences that will nonetheless remain between sinner and deity.[30]

Contrition, confession, and satisfaction thus amount to the three necessary stages of a speech-act in a cosmos within which all human activity may be understood as linguistic behavior. Contrition is a double movement of reading: setting the text of his soul against the Word and moved by faith *in* the Word and love *for* it, the sinner finds his own letter wanting, is sorry, and intends to write anew. Satisfaction is the double movement of this rewriting: it offers a new gesture meant to make up for the inadequacy of a previous erring one, and is in this both a cancellation of the old and a self-sacrificing supplement to it; at the same time, it is a gesture that can only succeed by virtue of God's antecedent faith *in* and love *for* humanity, as expressed by the offer and self-sacrifice of his own son, the new man who is both cancellation of and a supplement to the old. And confession, the middle step, is the perpetual acknowledgment that in the effort to do and say the truth, one always falls short; yet it is also an expression of hope in the one who takes away the sins and errors of the world.

Where the speech-acts of penance and irony most obviously differ is with regard to the being addressed by these self-canceling gestures: in the one case, infinite and consubstantial with the Word; in the other case, finite, and always at some temporal and conceptual distance from the speaker. Up to that point in the process, however, remarkable similarities exist. Both penance and irony amount to the acknowledgment (momentary or perpetual) that one's new reading shows one's previous writing to be in error; in fact, that even in the instant of writing, one's simultaneous reading acknowledges the gap between what one has said and what one would like to mean. Confessing this disparity, both the penitent and the ironist bow out of the text, saying, in effect, "Not my will, but thine. Not my intentions, but yours. I trust in the Word (or the word). Thy will be done." Thus the text is offered up as a sacrificial double, standing in place of the author and given over to the mercy of the hearer. When the hearer is God, the sacrifice is adequate and the author's intentions are saved, for the Lord God is truly a merciful hearer of speakers' utterances. Disappearing from the text, the author then enters the kingdom of heaven in which there is no dark mediation, no sacrifice, and no gap between letter and spirit.[31] But when one's hearer is not God, one's intentions may be utterly lost. Even then there is recompense of a sort, for the text—not having been an adequate sacrifice—endures, and in its place the literal hearer becomes a victim.

Between these extremes of complete success and abject failure, there is an ordinary, purgatorial world of authors and readers, tellers and hearers, the world upon which Chaucer concentrates in the bulk of the *Canterbury Tales*.[32] This is a world where there are many ironies, some identifiable ironists, and an uncertain number of genuine penitents. Though most of Chaucer's tellers succeed quite well in fulfilling at least their "literal" task of entertainment—even if not all the pilgrims are amused—it is a famously debated question how accurately these tales (and persons) conform to the spirit either of pilgrimage or of the figures and paradigms within and behind their telling, as well as how truly their auditors hear the tales, or judge the tellers, insofar as we can ascertain from their comments and the stories that they tell in turn.

Examples abound of this manifold difficulty in matching inside with outside, intention with reception, and spirit with letter. In the *Prologue*, there is gap after gap—whether satirically observed or not, it is hard to say—between what the pilgrims wear, do, and profess, and what a rigorous view of their estate, function, and present purpose might demand: one thinks, among many others, of the Prioress, the Monk, the Physician, and the Miller who leads the way to Canterbury with a bagpipe. As for the succeeding tales, if the Miller does not wholly misunderstand the Knight, he at least inverts his social superior's view of romantic love, which is either sympathetic or skeptical—depending on how one reads the tonal variations he works upon Boccaccio, and how deliberate or accidental these seem—but certainly "spiritual" by comparison with the Miller's fabliau (unless we read this allegorically). Though the Reeve takes the Miller's words in a circumstantially allegorical way, as deprecating his own carpenter's craft, and therefore as the occasion for a sermon against "ribaudye," which the Host cuts off as unfit for his estate, his own ensuing tale is no less fleshly and considerably less charitable in "quitting" than its predecessor. The Wife of Bath misapplies and probably misunderstands her textual authorities, takes only the flattering sense of her tale, and arguably misunderstands her own iconographic significance; yet the Clerk's view of good women and good marriage neither captures the Wife's "spirit" nor can serve as a better guide to the literal or spiritual conduct of men and women with each other (as opposed to their conduct with respect to God). The Pardoner correctly reads his own tale, but only for meaning; its significance escapes him, for he fails to grasp both the way it mirrors his own condition and its

likely impact on his audience's gullibility as they confront the
cupidity exemplified in both tale and teller. The Franklin tells a
tale which either puts a fine gloss on lust, mistaking social opinion
for truth, or celebrates the separate marital peace which Averagus
and Dorigen attain by outwardly acknowledging while inwardly
ignoring the conventional hierarchy—and semiotics—of man and
wife. Summoner and Friar taunt one another with problems of
glossing and literality; the Nun's Priest teases us with the relation
between fruit and chaff; and "Chaucer" poses with the tales of
Melibee and Thopas a stylistically coded version of the disjunction
between earnest and game that other tales have rendered problematic, but which reappears with renewed sharpness in the Parson's Tale, only to be somehow qualified again by the Retraction.

I propose no new interpretation of all these juxtapositions, of all
this riddling about the relationship between what someone means
by a text and what the text signifies in "itself," in the whole
contextual and intertextual fabric which is "Chaucer's" writing
and "our" reading, and vice versa. I only want to insist that these
juxtapositions are necessarily ironic. No one will doubt, of course,
that the *Canterbury Tales* are full of irony: that was evident to
Chaucer's earliest readers, so far as we can ascertain, even though
they might not have used quite our modern vocabulary.[33] Some of
the pilgrims are portrayed in a way that makes them seem to
practice irony themselves—most of us would count the Clerk, the
Pardoner, and the Nun's Priest among these—though not always in
a way that makes us confident that pre-Romantic persons regularly
confined themselves to stable ironies.[34] But the ironies which occur
as a consequence of the interaction between tale and tale, tale and
teller, tale and hearer, and fruit and chaff quite outrun the control
of any separate intender within Chaucer's fiction.

Indeed, most if not all of these latter ironies depend upon just
those aspects of the semiotic process which evade domination by
an individual speaker or writer. We laugh at the Pardoner, among
other reasons, just because he thinks he can confine the significance of his tale to bounds that will serve his own cupidity, and
because he misses the opportunity for an instructive self-reference
in his story of drinking, swearing, and gambling. We laugh at the
Reeve—or is it the Miller?—because he picks up a connection that
we—and the Miller?—might have missed, lacking the Reeve's
sense of injury. We laugh at the Host when he makes a literal
application of the Clerk's story of Walter and Griselda, not knowing ourselves just how to take the Clerk's very "spiritual" quitting

of the Wife's fleshly advocacy of women's dominance over men. And we laugh even at ourselves, confronting a challenge like the Nun's Priest's: hunting for fruit in the chickenyard seems altogether too earnest, yet to ignore tropological and anagogical resonances in Chauntecleer's escape from the fox is to allow ourselves to be victimized by a game of letters. And so on and so forth; no doubt every reader of Chaucer has favorite examples of the vertigo induced by the pilgrims'—and our—inability to control the wayward literality of these tales, and of our reading of them.

To control wayward literality—to keep ourselves from wandering by the way—would be to know how to guarantee the match between meaning and significance. When we, or someone else, mistakes that fit of inside and outside, irony has occurred; when the mistake is "intentional"—when the duped speaker or agent is a persona, a being within quotation marks—then "we" share in the joke at some other literal hearer's expense. But that kind of joking requires a carefully controlled context, a context much more carefully controlled than the larger business of life—or pilgrimage, or the relation between spirit and flesh—usually permits. And even in controlled contexts, there is always that troubling dialectic of blindness and insight: in order to say one thing (with the Wife, that the flesh is good, with the Clerk, that the flesh must submit) we ignore another. Since signification puts a "cut" into the order of things, we can never say it all; so we are always liable to irony, and if we are wise, we will therefore always express ourselves with a certain reserve.

While on pilgrimage, however, we must perforce express ourselves. Since one's every act carries some significance, even apart from one's intentions, it is not possible to keep silence. So pilgrims speak, whether with the intention of meeting Harry Bailey's challenge or of making penitential satisfaction in that third way which the Parson names: "yevynge of good conseil and comfort, goostly and bodily" (1029). It seems natural, given the whole context of the *Canterbury Tales*, to think of counsel and comfort as the "true" sentence—the ultimate significance—of sentence and solace: if someone understands being on pilgrimage, he or she should *mean* the performing of Harry Bailey's game to have that earnest, to serve as a satisfaction in speaking that will complement the satisfaction in doing which is going on pilgrimage. Whether many—or any—of the pilgrims really mean their tales in this way depends, of course, on who hears them: only a divine auditor could be sure, could so aid in the speaking as to foster an earnest will, and so supplement

the text as to ensure an earnest effect. The rest of us will inevitably differ.

We will differ most of all because of the problem about which so many pilgrims give counsel and comfort—or correct the counsel and comfort given by others. No doubt it would be over-bold to argue that all the tales have a single subject. But given the context I have been working up here, I think it fair to claim that within their various subjects many of the pilgrims find themselves trying to give counsel and comfort about the (wayward) letter, what to do with it, how to cope with its vagaries. Of course the particular letter is always different, for these are particular "persons" of different stations, sexes, moral lives, insights, and qualities of mind. Each offering of counsel and comfort, being finite and particular, therefore leaves something out. But the problem addressed stays surprisingly constant, whether it is the Monk's "How shal the world be served?" or Dame Alys's seemingly less general question about what to do with one's "sely instrument," or the Franklin's question about the letter and spirit of marriage, or the Miller's rude reminder of the letter that underlies courtly love-talk, or the Man of Law's warning that letters—and "joye of this world"—stray and change, except as Christ sees fit to preserve us.

Most of the pilgrims seem quite confident of their ability to get right the relation between letter and spirit. Even those speakers who set us a difficult puzzle in these matters—like the Clerk and the Nun's Priest—still assure us that a solution can be had, that we can take our pleasure and yet attain the fruit of the tale. Even the Pardoner, while doubting our ability to get things right, never doubts his own powers to keep them right for him. Only one pilgrim professes real doubt: that enigmatic "Chaucer" who goes on this pilgrimage and sets down everyone's words with the faithfulest care for the letter but with a remarkably uncertain sense for which sentence is best. "Chaucer" on pilgrimage, when pressed by the Host, offers two tales. The first tale is of Sir Thopas; it is "a rym I lerned longe agoon," and all that he can provide when asked for a "tale of myrth" (*Thopas* VII, 709, 706). No tale could come closer to being all letter and no spirit. It is a brilliantly mindless display of rule-governed performance, with no ideas in it worth the mention: as the Host says, it is "verray lewednesse" and "drasty ryming" that is "nat worth a toord." Prevented from merriment, "Chaucer" offers instead "a litel thyng in prose," "a moral tale vertuous" which has been "told somtyme in sondry wyse / Of sondry folk" (*Thopas*, 941–42). "Chaucer" will tell it in his own way, but no matter; like each of the four evangelists, he will offer the same sentence as all the other tellers of this tale, "Al be ther in hir tellyng difference" (*Thopas*, 948). And sure enough, the *Tale of Melibee* turns out to be as close to pure cognitive as a tale can be; it is a transparent allegory recommending the virtue of patience. Ironically enough, this is just the virtue that most of us lack in reading both Thopas and Melibee, though it is also just the virtue which our Host wants to recommend to his wife, who like Noah's wife, is clearly a comic figure of the impatient, outraged flesh itself, punishing anything that shows either too little spirit or too much.

"Chaucer's" then, is the extreme ironic response to the irony posed by the mismatch between letter and spirit: a pretended denial—how much pretended, we cannot say—that he can ever fit chaff and fruit together in a way that preserves both solace and sentence, at least on the same plane. There are lesser versions of a similar irony of incapacity in "Chaucer's" almost random commentary on tellers and tales—his agreement with the Monk's opinion of Augustine, his withdrawal into orthodox revulsion at the Miller's churlishness—and there are the constructed, motivating ironies which come from "his" juxtaposing of one tale with another.[35] But none of these ironies permits us to say where "Chaucer" stands: by insisting on his own incapacity at the task which others take on so recklessly, he leaves us on our own with "other" people's words and no sure guide to his intentions in recording them. Playfully sacrificing his authority through this sort of irony long before he sacrifices it in literal earnest through the Retraction, "Chaucer" forces us to hunt elsewhere for a standard of judgment.

We can say nonetheless that conventions and common sense allow us to move somewhat further toward judgment than this "Chaucer." Indeed, "his" irony—the irony that arises throughout the *Canterbury Tales*—very much alerts us to our dependence on common sense and convention, which is a dependence on the word in its lower-case sense. That is to say, irony makes us realize how much we need the whole community of speakers whose collective performative acts constitute that always absent *langue* which guarantees the workings and the cognitive potential of each "present" *parôle*. It is this word—which we dwell within, yet cannot fully know—which guarantees our likeness to one another; and it is our individual use and understanding of this word which makes us deviate from one another: thus full synonymy is no more possible than it is for two persons to occupy the same place at the same time. We therefore always stand in metaphoric relationship to one another, along with our reading and writing, which can never transcend metaphor. The cognitive apprehension of this metaphoric unity in the word guarantees significance, enabling a mutual though faulty recognition which must stand first in the order of epistemology. Yet ontologically, in the actual deed of reading and writing the performative comes first. One must speak before one's words can be converted to objects of knowledge, whether for oneself, for another, or for that God who will not recognize a faith unvivified by charity, an inwardness not expressed in some activity.[36]

To put it another way, insofar as we know at all, metaphor—which is *signum tantum*, pure sign—comes first; but in the ontological moment of reading, living, and writing, the priority goes to synecdoche, which is both *signum et res*, both a sign and an intentional, actual, though from the mortal point of view finally unknowable, connection of one thing with another. And these two moments stand in mutually deconstructable tension. Every pretense at the metaphoric totalization of one's grasp on the world can be broken down into associative relationships of the contingent parts within an unrealizable, unstatable, but all-encompassing context. But to name this context, which we must if we are to grasp it and act within it, requires another deconstructive turn toward metaphor.[37] And so on and so forth. Though every attempt at knowing thus yields a fall, there is redemptive consolation in recognizing our limitative contingency: synecdochically related to the word, each reader and writer shows himself to be a member of that whole community of speakers and their speaking which might be "mystically" understood as either the Body of Christ or *la langue*. In our performance, we are as the parts also the instruments of that whole syntactic and semantic system which every utterance synecdochically implies. But to acknowledge oneself as instrumental rather than original, and as partial rather than whole—as prolonged encounters with irony should inspire us to do—is again to confess one's insufficiency, to intend what good one can and to cast oneself into the unknowable arms of language, and the good will of one's hearers.

Thus one's words and the whole context in which one lives never catch up with each other: one's words are universal, but disembodied; one's life particular, mortal, and signifying in ways that one knows too little about. Here is where the paradoxical affinity between irony and penance seems to break down, or better, to break apart into an irresolvable oscillation between different semiotic systems, each one standing in relation to the other again as performative to cognitive, and each therefore partly blind to the other. From one point of view, penance—since it involves the whole person and his or her place in the Book of Life—seems to be the superior and inclusive system. It not only involves more of the person than mere language, but it also serves in the most literal sense as the performative ground of right intentions that Christian plain speaking and good deeds should make manifest. As the ultimate confession of fault, penance simply confirms and completes the irony of insufficiency which Chaucer has implicitly and explicitly enacted throughout the *Canterbury Tales*. And given its divine hearer, whose grace enables in true penance an otherwise impossible conjunction of word and deed, meaning and significance, *signum tantum* and *signum et res*, penance achieves a communicative perfection denied to ordinary speech.

Yet so long as we remain pilgrims—that is to say, persons who do not yet know and speak face to face—we must always present ourselves to others (and to ourselves) in ordinary language, which is to say in an indirect and imperfect fashion, always open to misconstruction. Since words can never touch or iconically "fit" that to which they refer, nor be used in ways that fully control the wayward letter, there is always a gap between what we mean and what we say, a gap crossed only by the hearer's tenuous good will and sense of propriety. If what we mean has to do not just with words, but with the connection between letter and spirit—with the range of that problem that runs from the relation between game and earnest to the relation between fleshly existence and its inward reflection of the divine Image—then the gap is redoubled, appearing once in the medium and once in the topic, as well as at their juncture. Irony is not the only response to this imperfection— parable and allegory will also serve to acknowledge, imitate, and guard against some of its effects—nor are all ironies as self-effacing and ultimately generous as "Chaucer's." But some such response seems necessary if one is aware of the limits of human speech. Or rather, if we think that our deeds have significance as well as our words, two such responses seem necessary: one for our fellows, one for a hearer who cannot mistake the whole context nor be deceived about intentions. Knowing and doing, words and deeds, even irony and penance: so long as we remain textual and fleshly, the oscillation cannot end.

Reed College

NOTES

1. In preparing the final version of this essay, I have greatly profited from conversations with Ronald Herzman, Christine Knodt, and Charles Svitavsky, and from the comments of Mary Carruthers and Patricia Eberle. For reviews of the rather extensive literature on Chaucer's Retraction, see James D. Gordon, "Chaucer's Retraction: A Review of Opinion," in *Studies in Honor of A. C. Baugh*, ed. MacEdward Leach (Philadelphia: University of Pennsylvania Press, 1961), pp. 81–96; and Rodney Delasanta, "Penance and Poetry in the *Canterbury Tales*," *PMLA* 93 (1978), 240–47. Delasanta's survey and independent conclusions bear out Gordon's claim that the "general trend today" is "toward recognizing the Retraction as authentic . . . and toward explaining it as a matter of conscience rather than of aesthetics" (p. 91).

2. These intuitively self-evident statements depend upon principles of hermeneutic theory which are most lucidly explored by David Couzens Hoy, *The Critical Circle* (Berkeley and Los Angeles: University of California Press, 1978). For a more formal justification of the underlying proposition that semantics takes logical priority over syntax (as therefore does the cognitive over the performative), see David Holdcroft, *Words and Deeds* (Oxford: Clarendon Press, 1978). In arguing that illocutionary acts can only be understood within a context of relevant circumstances and therefore only with some reference to a speaker's denotative intentions, Holdcroft arrives by way of Anglo-Saxon philosophical stategies at a position remarkably like that which Paul Ricoeur reaches by way of the competing continental tradition, both French and German. See Paul Ricoeur, *Interpretation Theory: Discourse and the Surplus of Meaning* (Fort Worth: Texas Christian University Press, 1976).

3. For arguments about the inherent unpredictability and continual fluidity of semiotic systems, see Umberto Eco, *A Theory of Semiotics* (Bloomington: Indiana University Press, 1976). The proposition that sign-making is radically playful, and therefore radically "deconstructive" of both historicity and science can be found throughout the work of Jacques Derrida and his epigones. See especially *Writing and Difference*, trans. Alan Bass (Chicago: University of Chicago Press, 1978), pp. 292–93.

4. *Parson's Tale*, Fragment X, 57. Where further line references seem useful, they will appear parenthetically in my text, all with reference to John H. Fisher, ed., *The Complete Poetry and Prose of Geoffrey Chaucer* (New York: Holt, Rinehart, and Winston, 1977).

5. Several critics emphasize the implicit leap here from one order of reality to another. For examples, see Peter Elbow, *Oppositions in Chaucer* (Middletown, Conn.: Wesleyan University Press, 1975), pp. 133–34; Donald R. Howard, *The Idea of the Canterbury Tales* (Berkeley and Los Angeles: University of California Press, 1976), p. 179; and Robert O. Payne, *The Key of Remembrance* (New Haven, Conn.: Yale University Press, 1963), p. 89.

6. The strong and controversial thesis identifying Chaucer's intentions with St. Paul's may be found in D. W. Robertson, Jr., *A Preface to Chaucer* (Princeton, N. J.: Princeton University Press, 1962), esp. p. 369.

7. Among those who deplore the orthodoxy and try to circumscribe the impact of the Retraction are Charles Owen, *Pilgrimage and Storytelling in the Canterbury Tales: The Dialectic of "Ernest and Game"* (Norman: University of Oklahoma Press, 1977), esp. pp. 6, 29; and Stephen Knight, "Chaucer and the Sociology of Literature," in *Studies in the Age of Chaucer*, ed. Roy J. Pearcy, vol. 2 (Norman: University of Oklahoma Press, 1980), pp. 15–51.

8. Alfred David, *The Strumpet Muse* (Bloomington: Indiana University Press, 1976), p. 290.

9. E. D. Hirsch, *Validity in Interpretation* (New Haven, Conn.: Yale University Press, 1967).

10. My argument depends upon a long analytic tradition about the nature of irony. Four of the most influential works are: Søren Kierkegaard, *The Concept of Irony*, trans. Lee M. Capel (Bloomington: Indiana University Press, 1968); Kenneth Burke, *A Grammar of Motives and a Rhetoric of Motives*, (Cleveland: Meridian Books, 1962), esp. 402–503; D. C. Muecke, *The Compass of Irony* (London: Methuen, 1969); and Wayne C. Booth, *A Rhetoric of Irony* (Chicago: University of Chicago Press, 1974).

11. Any edition of the Catholic Encyclopedia will give a fairly reliable history of penitential theory and practice, though one must beware of its Thomistic bias. More balanced and extensive treatments may be found in Alfred Vacant and E. Mangenot, eds., *Dictionnaire de théologie catholique*, (Paris, 1909–1950), vol. 12, pt. 1, cols. 948–1054; and Thomas N. Tentler, *Sin and Confession on the Eve of the Reformation* (Princeton, N. J.: Princeton University Press, 1977). The most useful study of medieval penance known to me is Reinhard Schwartz, *Vorgeschichte der Reformatorischen Busstheologie* (Berlin: Walter de Gruyter and Company, 1968). For Chaucer's own understanding of penance, the *Parson's Tale* is our only explicit evidence, though the pilgrimage motif itself, and certain other tales—especially the *Pardoner's Tale*—imply a wide and specific knowledge of penitential theology.

12. Isidore of Seville, *Etymologiarum sive originum*, ed. W. M. Lindsay (Oxford: Clarendon Press, 1911), 6.39–40. My analysis of penitential semiotics derives mainly from St. Augustine, esp. *On Christian Doctrine*, trans. D. W. Robertson, Jr. (Indianapolis: Bobbs–Merrill, 1958), bk. 3, pp. 78–117. I rely heavily on R. A. Markus, "St. Augustine on Signs," *Phronesis* 2 (1957), 60–83; and Marcia L. Colish, *The Mirror of Language: A Study in the Medieval Theory of Knowledge* (New Haven, Conn.: Yale University Press, 1968). In the attempt to suggest affinities between medieval and modern theories of signs, I have especially profited from Eugene Vance, "Mervelous Signals: Poetics, Sign Theory, and Politics in Chaucer's *Troilus*," *New Literary History* 10 (1979), 293–337; and Juri M. Lotman, "Problems in the Typology of Culture," in *Soviet Semiotics*, ed. and trans. Daniel P. Lucid (Baltimore: The Johns Hopkins University Press, 1977), pp. 213–21.

13. This common formula may be found in Peter Lombard, *Sententiarum libri quatuor* IV.4.1, in *Patrologiae cursus completus: Series Latina*, ed. J. P. Migne, vol. 192, col. 846. See also the discussion in St. Thomas Aquinas, *Summa Theologiae* 3a.62.1. In my reference to St. Thomas, I use the Blackfriars edition and translation (New York: McGraw–Hill, 1963–75), vols. 56 and 60, and am indebted to the notes and appendices by David Bourke, Reginald Masterson, and T. C. O'Brien.

14. See Rosamond Tuve, *Allegorical Imagery*, (Princeton, N. J.: Princeton University Press, 1966), esp. pp. 57–143.

15. For this point, and for the argument that the tale is Chaucer's deliberate cancellation of all that has gone before, see Lee W. Patterson, "The 'Parson's Tale' and the Quitting of the 'Canterbury Tales,'" *Traditio* 34 (1978), 331–80.

16. In earlier works—the *Parliament of Fowles*, the *House of Fame*, and *Troilus*, Chaucer depicts himself as a reader and interpreter of texts, one who is at pains to follow authority and yet pained by the vagaries of changing tongues, imperfect transmission, defective capacities, and shifting perspectives. His discourse on rumor in the *House of Fame* could well serve as a medieval lament on the effects of

Derrida's notion of dissemination. For the *Canterbury Tales* themselves, many of us (following the lead of D. W. Robertson, among others) find it second nature to speak of the pilgrims as readers—often as misreaders—of their tales, their stations, and of this occasion for storytelling. Both in the narrow sense of performing and interpreting a text and in the larger sense of working through signs to acquire understanding—of oneself, of others' intentions, of the patterns in all sorts of reality—reading thus comes to stand as one of the main organizing topics, perhaps the central organizing topic, of Chaucer's final work.

17. Paul de Man, *Blindness and Insight* (New York: Oxford University Press, 1971).

18. Tentler, *Sin and Confession,* pp. 281–302.

19. St. Thomas, *ST*, vol. 60, appendix I, pp. 175–79. Cf. Peter Lombard, *Sent.,* IV.22.3, *PL* 192, col. 899.

20. Quoted in Peter Lombard, *Sent.,* IV.14.1, *PL* 192, col. 869. See the analysis of this commonplace in Peter the Chanter, *Verbum Abbreviatum, PL,* vol. 205, col. 346: "Continue dolendum est de peccato, quod declarat ipsa dictionis virtus. Poenitentia enim est poenam tenere, ut semper puniat, in se ulciscendo, quod commisit peccando. Ille poenam tenet, qui semper vindicat, quod commisisse dolet. Poenitentia igitur est vindicta semper puniens in se quod commisisse dolet." Cf. the analogous formula quoted in the *Parson's Tale:* "Penitence is the waymentynge of man that sorweth for his synne and pyneth hymself for he hath mysdoon"(84).

21. The theological complexities of the movement from the obscured divine image to the restored, active likeness are best laid out by Robert Javelet, *Image et ressemblance au douzième siècle de St. Anselme à Alain de Lille* (Paris: Letouzey et Ané, 1967).

22. Or as the Parson puts it, penitence (in its first part, contrition) "destroyeth the prisoun of helle; and maketh wayk and fieble alle the strengthes of the develes; and restoreth the yiftes of the Hooly Goost and of alle goode vertues. And it clenseth the soule of synne, and delivereth the soule fro the peyne of helle, and fro the compaignye of the devel, and fro the servage of synne, and restoreth it to alle goodes espirituels, and to the compaignye and communyoun of Hooly Chirche" (310–11).

23. These terms derive from the speech-act theories of J. L. Austin and John R. Searle. Their literary implications are most fully developed in Mary Louise Pratt, *Toward a Speech Act Theory of Literary Discourse,* (Bloomington: Indiana University Press, 1977).

24. See Holdcroft, *Words and Deeds,* pp. 131–70.

25. In other words, cooperative grace produces synergistic effects. See Schwartz, *Vorgeschichte,* p. 38.

26. The Parson gets at this deformation with other figures: sin bereaves man of natural and spiritual goods (249); it turns good order upside down (262).

27. See, for example, the Macro moral *Mankind,* line 742, in *The Macro Plays,* ed. Mark Eccles, E.E.T.S., o.s. 262 (London: Oxford University Press, 1969). The Parson follows this usage in lines 146–74, 249, 262, and 475–92 (in the last of these, for instance, he describes envy as a sin against kind).

28. The growing awareness of this difficulty contributed to the increasing emphasis placed on attritionist theories of penance in the later Middle Ages. Attrition seems to be the penitential counterpart of the Franciscan doctrine of *facere quod in se est:* less than perfect sorrow; it nevertheless suffices to win grace. For the development of attritionist theories of penance, see Tentler, *Sin and Confession,* pp. 250–300.

29. This Pauline doctrine lies behind Augustine's notion that penance is motivated both by fear and by love. The necessity of such a double compunction, and the consequent uncertainty about one's acceptablity to God, finds further emphasis in Gregory the Great, and in the Catholic tradition thereafter. See Schwartz, *Vorgeschichte*, esp. pp. 70–79.

30. Derrida's convention of placing the "trace" (and many forms of the copula) "under erasure" is analyzed by Gayatri Chakravorty Spivak in the preface to her translation of *Of Grammatology* (Baltimore: The Johns Hopkins University Press, 1976), pp. xv–xvii. As she observes, Derrida's practice derives (and differs) from Heidegger's trick of crossing out "Being." Of course there is no point in arguing that Chaucer anticipates Derridean attacks on metaphysics. I would, however, want to argue that Derrida's strategies grow out of the very tradition from which he would distance himself, especially from those places in the tradition which emphasize paradoxes of communication, exemplification, and revelation.

31. See St. Thomas, *ST* Ia.15.3, ad 1.

32. With speakers and hearers, the issue is strictly speaking a question of contextuality as well as intertextuality. My analysis of these matters depends implicitly upon that of H. P. Grice, e.g., his "Utterer's Meaning, Sentence-Meaning, and Word-Meaning," in *The Philosophy of Language*, ed. J. R. Searle (London: Oxford University Press, 1971), pp. 54–70. I am grateful to George Bealer for his elucidation of Grice's strategy.

33. I believe that the earliest survey of premodern reactions to Chaucer's irony is Earle Birney, "Is Chaucer's Irony a Modern Discovery," *JEGP* 41 (1942), 303–19.

34. The term "stable irony" is Wayne Booth's, whose *Rhetoric of Irony* (p.235) agrees with D. C. Muecke's *Compass of Irony* in finding little or no undecidable irony until at least the eighteenth century.

35. Of course the order of the fragments remains debatable, as must therefore the intentionality of some of these juxtapositional ironies.

36. As this point applies in speech-act theory, I am indebted for some clarification to my colleague, William Ray. For its theological formulation, see St. Thomas, *ST* 31.85.6, rep 1, obj.1. As Artur Landgraf observes, the distinction between the action of grace and the action of charity—which seems to me to be the underlying distinction in Aquinas' thought about penance—is one that St. Bonaventura also makes, and which ultimately has to do with the difference between the order of formal causes and the order of material causes. "Grundlagen für ein Verständnis der Busslehre der Früh-und Hochscholastik," *Zeitschrift für Katholische Theologie* 51 (1927), 193. Though the scholastics would surely disapprove of anyone's reducing this difference to that between the cognitive and the performative, I think that they would recognize our mutually implicative binarism as a version of their own, which has finally to do with the interaction between the Word and deeds.

37. For an extended and rather more skeptical argument to this effect (without, of course, the attempt to make contact with medieval categories of thought), see Paul de Man, *Allegories of Reading* (New Haven, Conn.: Yale University Press, 1979).

Deconstruction and Renaissance Literature

Gary F. Waller

ouis Althusser once suggested that our age would be looked back to as one in which the most fundamental human activities—speaking, writing, perceiving—were radically revalued.[1] Even in the hermetic world of the literary academy and in the dark (and, to many of us, still warm and comforting) inner room of Renaissance scholarship, there have been glimmerings recently of a dazzling and disturbing light. What has been variously, triumphantly, provocatively, even fearfully, termed a new philosophical paradigm, a revolution in perception, or a subversion of the truths of Western humanism, has entered (or perhaps broken down) our doors. But let me abandon my metaphor before it abandons me and state what has gradually become commonplace—that not since the late eighteenth century have the role and status of interpretation, its relation to history, to reading and writing, been put so fiercely and fundamentally in question. What impact, I want to ask in this essay, might these disturbances have on our long-peaceful realm of Renaissance studies?

In particular, I want to ask what we may learn or appropriate from Jacques Derrida and his French, English, and American progeny. Deconstruction, Derrida's adaptation of the Heideggerian question, has developed into such a powerful critique of traditional metaphysics' reification of the sign and the process of signification, and of such concepts as causality, identity, truth, and subject, that, at the very least, as Gerald Graff notes, "whatever one's reservations about it, deconstructionist criticism has given professional literary studies . . . something to fight about."[2] It is clear as well that, whether we like it or not, deconstruction *works*, powerfully and disturbingly. A fundamental problem for literary studies today,

69

especially for literary history, is to fight through its powerful challenge. Whether we see it as a detour or a freeway, all serious readers of literature are being directed through the deconstructive route. So my focus in this essay will be: how are the deconstructive questions applicable to our readings of Renaissance literature? What distinctive problems for the reading of Renaissance texts do we discover? What residual resistances to the deconstructive questions do we, as Renaissance scholars, inherit? To what extent can we see the Renaissance fascination with language—with both its apparent plenitude and its frustrating emptiness—as raising the kinds of questions that, Derrida insists, always already lie within textuality? Can we ignore what Terry Eagleton calls deconstruction's "hair-raising radicalism—the nerve and daring with which it knocks the stuffing out of every smug concept," or its urge to think the unthinkable (at least for Renaissance scholars) that we must, in Vincent Leitch's words, "subvert without pity the obvious and stubborn referentiality" of the text?[3] Of Shakespeare? we all want to ask. Of Sidney? Of Spenser?

I will start by trying to construct a way into assessing the challenge deconstruction poses. To date, with few exceptions, Renaissance scholarship has remained stubbornly unaffected by its tremors. Michael McCanles notes that while in many areas of literary history "the old debate" between New Criticism and Old Historicism has been transformed or blurred, Renaissance scholarship remains "generally blind to the theoretical and methodological problems raised by its canonized approaches to its own material."[4] At a conference on Sidney, even so mildly revisionist a study as Richard McCoy's fine book was greeted by puzzlement, misapprehension, or (a more hopeful sign) plain indignation.[5] With some notable but rare exceptions—Stephen Greenblatt's work on Renaissance self-fashioning, Jonathan Goldberg's deconstructive readings of Spenser, or some of the essays in the Sidney number of *Studies in the Literary Imagination*, for example—Renaissance scholarship remains suspended in its traditional "natural" assumptions about "meaning," "text," "source," "author," "reading"—all concepts that have been central to more than two decades of intense debate in many other areas of literary theory and practice.[6] Much work in the Renaissance remains, for instance, author-centered to the point of hagiography, ingenuously reflectionist, tied to the assertion that there are "objective," historically verifiable readings, and to discussions of influences, sources, and parallels. The reading of Renaissance texts is still primarily seen as an investigative procedure designed to locate their origins in particular events or documents of their writers' lives, or to recover fixed or "authentic" Renaissance meanings. There is, in short, little awareness that our most basic conceptions of literary history and criticism have been so radically challenged—and certainly not only by deconstruction— that some fundamental adjustments are required unless we are simply content to take refuge in a nostalgic antiquarianism.

To fill out the details and assess this challenge, we might usefully start with Jacques Derrida and his American followers. As Tilottama Rajan summarizes him (never an easy task), Derrida characteristically uses the term "deconstruction" to initiate a "procedure of textual analysis by which the critic dismantles or takes apart the paraphrasable meaning of a text, in order to disclose within that text the gaps in logic which reveal the author's subconscious awareness of a commitment to a system of assumptions opposite to the one he explicitly endorses," and so challenge the unequivocal authority of any particular mode of signifying, any privileged reading, that seems to be produced by the text.[7] As Derrida's American followers tirelessly repeat, the critic—in thus revealing the latent metaphysical structure of the text—does not dismantle the text so much as demonstrate that it is already dismantled: "it performs on itself the act of deconstruction without any help from the critic."[8]

Accustomed, as we are, to looking to what we still habitually call "texts" for coherent and consistent meanings, it seems uncomfortable to be made to focus on the "warring forces of signification" and to recognize, by means of what Derrida terms a "breakthrough," the "text's" inherent vulnerability. Is its apparent desire for truth inevitably hollow and self-defeating? The deconstructive critic seizes on what he perceives as the telltale lines of breakage or fissure. In Hartman's provocative metaphor, he "reaps" the text to show those points where it contradicts itself. The critic moves around inside the text, probing incompatibilities between grammar and rhetoric, pitting figure against concept and argument, subverting confident statement, and arguing that only by ignoring such contradictions can we sustain the illusion of representation, since all texts undo any system of meaning to which they seem to adhere. Texts exist in a continual state of play (in both the festive and mechanical senses of "play"). Within any apparently replete discourse—that is, where an illusion of meaning or presence is confidently maintained—there are always other discourses that contradict it.[9] Thus Jonathan Goldberg, in his reading of *The Faerie*

Queene, writes: "I do not aim at interpretation or fulfillment, but, rather, at describing the narrative principles that induce frustration, that deny closure," and which produce "a broken text."[10]

Nor, in most versions of deconstruction, can the reader take refuge in any fixed extratextual point of authority—in author, world vision, history, or any concept of the "real." A text, writes Roland Barthes—on this issue, if not all, deconstruction's ally—is no longer conceived of as "a line of words realising a single 'theological' message (the 'message' of the Author-God) but a multidimensional space in which a variety of writings, none of them original, blend and clash." The representational claim that saying and meaning coincide is, in Derrida's view, thus shattered: what a text presents us with, he asserts, is the unstable result of an effaced and continual struggle, one which did not cease when the text was encoded but remains "active and stirring, inscribed in white ink, an invisible drawing covered over in the palimpsest." "White Mythology," from which Derrida's remark is taken, is one of his most profound essays and deserves pondering by historicist critics, a matter I shall return to when I discuss history later in this essay. The Freudian insistence on consciousness as a palimpsest is transferred to the literary text elsewhere by Derrida. In "Freud and the Scene of Writing" he uses the metaphor of a magic writing pad—the child's toy made of a dark waxed base, a tissue, and the cellophane on which we write. We erase our writing, but it is nonetheless engraved in the writing block—and likewise the text is constituted not only by inscriptions but also by erasures whose presence continues to disturb and disrupt the surface plenitude.[11] A text is thus perceived less as an observable fixed, limited, object-in-the-world, and more as a network of preexistent traces, a weave of many textures.

At this point I might indulge in some preliminary deconstruction of my own. First, given our culture's residual beliefs about language as a medium of intention, we should note deconstruction's challenge to the dominant post- Renaissance assumption (Derrida would be happier with seeing it inherent in the Greek initiation of Western logocentrism) that language is a medium transparent to "things" and "concepts." We can (if I can inexcusably lump together thinkers and movements in profound opposition on many points) relate deconstruction to such developments as the Saussurian revolution in linguistics, or the Husserlian-Heideggerian concern with hermeneutics (developed subsequently in different ways by Ricoeur, say, or Gadamer). Deconstruction sees language as functioning only as differentiated signs, at once pointing to and yet radically subverting the possibility of transcendent meaning. Every sign is interpretable only by other signs. What Derrida terms "dissemination" is inherent in writing, pointing only to the undecidability of meaning, the "endless substitution and deferral" of characters and events to which Goldberg points in *The Faerie Queene.*[12]

But while part of the distinctiveness of deconstruction is explicable by the force of post-Saussurian linguistics, its increasingly visible power in the academy, especially in America, is perhaps understood only in relation to broader cultural forces. The Derridean abyss has been plunged eagerly into by a number of influential and at times brilliantly suggestive critics often known (albeit inaccurately) as the "Yale critics." Derrida cannot be held responsible for any of his disciples' plunderings and appropriations, and it is fascinating to watch how American deconstruction has focused on those aspects of the Derridean problematic which lend themselves to uncannily easy assimilation into the hegemonous American literary theory and pedagogy since the 1930s, New Criticism.

My tissue of quotations—an attempt to introduce some of the ways deconstruction might intervene in the discourse which still dominates Renaissance scholarship—has until now not raised the question of the discontinuities and distortions amongst deconstructive critics themselves, and in particular the distinctive direction deconstruction has acquired in America. We may appreciate the force of Jonathan Culler's assertion that "when deconstruction comes to America a shift takes place" by noting that the history of innovations in American criticism in the past fifty years has been predominantly one of partial and largely unsuccessful attempts to replace or supplement New Criticism.[13] Especially when we read disarming claims like Hillis Miller's that deconstruction is neither nihilism nor metaphysics but simply "interpretation as such . . . [an] untangling by way of the close reading of texts," deconstruction looks suspiciously like American formalism's last stand.[14] On the surface, of course, there are formidable differences: for New Criticism, the text is a complex but organic harmony; for deconstruction, a text is a plurality, its contradictions and polysemy disrupting any pretense at organic unity. Yet deconstruction can be construed as burrowing more deeply into text than the linguistic repertoire of New Criticism allowed. In what can be perceived as a ferocious extension of close reading, the deconstructive critic attends closely to the interstices and repressed shadows of the text's words. As Harold Bloom suggests, it seems at times that Brooks or Abrams and Miller or de Man are only arguing about *degrees* of irony: "deconstructive praxis," as he puts it, "in reading a poem, looks more and more like a refinement upon, but not a break with, the well-wrought Cleanth Brooks."[15]

Further deconstructing deconstruction's claim to break radically with formalism, we may note other similarities. Like New Criticism, deconstruction holds strong views on the so-called representational claims of literature. The rejection of extralinguistic presence, the suspicion of any reading that makes a text derive from a preliterary event of which it is always a deferred shadow, and assertions that inherent in literary language is an impossibility that sign and meaning can ever coincide, are all strangely akin to New Criticism's insistence on the self-contained nature of the literary artifact. Goldberg, for instance, rejects any approach to *The Faerie Queene* that refers it "to some other system of supposedly stable and finally reductive sets of meanings,"[16] an unusual stance (to put it mildly) in the context of traditional Spenser studies, but one which is explicable in the context of American formalism and its appropriation of the deconstructive urgency. Among American deconstructionists, Derrida's *il n'y a pas de hors-texte* is widely read as an insistence that we can never escape from the text rather than as an assertion that text, or textuality, is everywhere, that there is nothing other than text.[17] In American deconstruction, the Derridean questioning of margins and boundaries is subtly neutralized into a convenient, and familiar, pedagogy, that there is nothing beyond the text and its interstices, gaps, and indeterminacies. In short, while—as I will go on to concede—deconstruction should certainly make us reflect on the very foundation of our discipline, we must also recognize its historical place—that in America at least it has become all too easily assimilated by our residual New Criticism and that, perhaps, it is apocalyptic criticism in a peculiarly paranoid stage of our culture, or even, as Terry Eagleton cruelly taunts, the last place left for the liberal conscience to play.[18]

To place deconstruction within the cultural dynamics of our time is not, however, to dismantle it, least of all for Renaissance scholars. Indeed, it is not a little depressing to note the sighs of complacency from traditional Renaissance scholars who wish to avoid the Derridean questioning when they perceive the cultural process by which deconstruction has been unmasked and neutralized—as that Old Enemy besieging our embattled Castle of Historicism: New Criticism, only now in a trendy disguise. Hostile indignation can then be succeeded by calm patronization. But the power of deconstruction cannot, I believe, be dealt with as easily as many of its advocates or its opponents, in their different ways, would like. So far as Renaissance scholarship is concerned, we simply cannot return to the security blanket of Old Historicism. In what follows, therefore, I propose to suggest some ways in which the deconstructivist questions—especially as they overlap with or reinforce other poststructuralist concerns—do fundamentally challenge traditional Renaissance scholarship. In particular I want to focus on four loci where the challenge seems especially important—the concepts of *author, text, history,* and *reading.*

First then, to the author, what Roland Barthes terms "that somewhat decrepit deity of the old criticism,"[19] which, in an archaically hagiographic manner, still dominates much Renaissance criticism. Part of the deconstructive challenge is a questioning of the place of both authorial identity and authority within the inworming that Derrida finds at the heart of every text. But as my mention of Barthes (not to mention New Criticism itself) makes clear, the questioning of the place and power of the author over the text and the further questioning of the Cartesian transcendental subject are issues that have surfaced in a wide range of Western thought, from Nietzsche onward. In Foucault's words, "man" is "only a recent invention, a figure not yet two centuries old," and the valorization of individualism a metaphor whereby post-Renaissance man has protected himself from insignificance as if, as Shakespeare's Coriolanus puts it, "a man were author of himself."[20]

When it considers the role and authority of the author, however, the American version of deconstruction seems puzzlingly simplistic. Because of the residual New Critical proscription of the Intentional Fallacy, the irrelevance of the author's power over his text is widely taken for granted but rarely given especially vigorous philosophical questioning. But if we turn back to deconstruction's primary sources as well as to more recent developments in French poststructuralism, then something more profound and useful for Renaissance scholarship emerges. Even Barthes's remark that the author can, of course, "come back' into the Text," but "only as a guest,' so to speak,"[21] seems flippant and question-begging alongside the work of Althusser, Lacan, or Kristeva on the structured nature of the subject within textuality. Here Renaissance scholars need to learn both deeply and quickly how completely the poststructuralist emphasis on the "individual" as always already a subject of any discourse into which he finds himself thrown (if I can

adapt and pervert a Heideggerian commonplace) has radically un-
dermined the bland humanist idealization of the "individual." Subjects are themselves constructed by languages; the "personality"
itself is a text traversed and constituted by further discursive practices and requiring continual translation and rereading. Lacan's for-
mulations on the structuring of the unconscious, for example, give
real bite to the deconstructive insistence that on the level of the
literary text, any utterance contains constitutive gaps whereby,
because of the misalignment of signifier and signified, it communi-
cates more, or less, or something other, than what it intends. Without embracing wholeheartedly a Lacanian or Kristevan description
of the symbolic and semiotic structuring of the unconscious, we
can nonetheless see how in an American deconstructionist criticism like Hillis Miller's, because such matters are avoided, his
praxis is rendered more superficial and self-containing than it
might otherwise be.[22] In particular, we are thereby prohibited from
establishing suggestive relations between the literary text and the
"social" and the "authorial" texts, and thus from seeing them all
as part of the flow of textuality.

An author's relationship to the languages that traverse him is, I
suggest, more complex than allowed for by, on the one hand, traditional humanist scholarship, and on the other, most American versions of deconstruction. In Renaissance scholarship, it is especially
crucial to face this issue, since it is by the late sixteenth century
that the valorization of the individual has taken a recognizable
philosophical shape as the ideologically dominant mechanism by
which men and women are written (or, as the humanist would
prefer, write themselves) into the world. Derrida's famous formulation is a convenient starting-point:

> The writer writes *in* a language and *in* a logic whose proper
> system, laws, and life his discourse by definition cannot
> dominate absolutely. He uses them only by letting himself,
> after a fashion and up to a point, be governed by the system.
> And the reading must always aim at a certain relationship,
> unperceived by the writer, between what he commands and
> what he does not command of the patterns of the language
> that he uses.[23]

Or as Edward Said asks pertinently, "to what extent is a text so
discontinuous a series of pre-texts or subtexts as to beggar the idea
of the author as a simple producer?" "Producer" is a crucial word

here. In the passage just noted, Derrida goes on to say that the relationship between what the writer does and does not command is describable as "a signifying structure that critical reading should *produce.*"[24] "Production," seemingly, is an activity that includes reading and writing alike, and neither activity is conceivable as free, spontaneous, instinctive. The writing of Shakespeare or Sidney or Milton is not "free," not created by a uniquely creative sovereign power, the "genius" reified by humanist hagiography, but by language—the text belongs finally to language, which speaks through him. We write, but are ourselves always already written.

Now, obviously—or at least it ought to be obvious—to undermine the autonomy of the author as the final producer of and authority over the text is not to doubt either the existence of an author or the power of his writing. Jonathan Culler tries to salvage the "subject," arguing "he may no longer be the origin of meaning, but meaning must move through him," without clarifying how the "self" can at the same time be the product of textual systems which write him/her/it into the world and exercise choice, decision, and moral commitment. Culler's discomfort here is particularly characteristic of American poststructuralist critics. It is especially poignant to observe the unease on this issue of one particular American writer who, while firmly dissociating himself from deconstruction, nonetheless has contributed greatly to its praxis. I refer to Harold Bloom, who has repeatedly argued against the "humanistic loss we sustain if we yield up the authority . . . to the partisans of writing, to those like Derrida and Foucault who imply . . . that language by itself writes the poems and thinks."[25] Bloom's quarrel here is a revealing misreading of both Derrida and Foucault, one that we must be especially careful to note. Paradoxically, certain French and British versions of deconstruction allow for the author's power over his text and his readers, in a much more incisive way than conceived by the naive antihistoricism of New Criticism, not as a detached point of authority "outside" the text, but as a function of the text itself. Let me explain. To situate the subject within discourse is certainly to adopt a polemical stance in the struggle against the vestiges of a residual and still powerful philosophical idealism. But it is more: it is to focus more precisely on the ways we all, as writers or readers, write ourselves into the world, on the authority we assume by participating in discursive structures, and (especially relevant to Renaissance studies) on how the notion of the author became, and has remained since the sixteenth century, a powerful functional principle within Western culture. In the Petrarchan sonnet sequence, for example, the author is very clearly the articulator of a rhetoric rather than its originator, and although there is often an identifiable individual scriptor, it normally seems to be the voice of a collectivity with which the poem's individual voice speaks. Renaissance sonnets remain notorious for trapping enthusiastic readers into biographical effusion, and we can learn much from Foucault's insistence on the author simply as the name we give to the locus of discursive forces, a temporarily "privileged moment of individuation." His point that the reification of such a locus has come to "impede the free circulation, the free manipulation, the free composition, decomposition, and recomposition of texuality" is amply evident in modern Renaissance scholarship.[26]

In discussing, albeit briefly, the author in Renaissance texts, I have noted that however powerful it may be, the deconstructive question (especially in its American form) is coerced by its residual relationship to New Criticism and thus itself requires deconstruction with the help of its French fathers. The same point applies to my next topic, the nature and status of *text*. What used to be taken for granted, the autonomy and monumentality of the literary object, has also been under attack from a diversity of viewpoints. The text is now variously described as a process, not a fixed object; as subsumed beneath intertextual relations; as an infinitely shifting and deceptive assemblage of traces, inhabited by discourses that contradict or undermine its seeming solidity. So insistent are the attacks that it is difficult to avoid concluding that we are seeing a major revaluation of a curiously long-lasting mystification in our cultural history. Derrida speaks neatly of the text as an "assemblage," a bringing together of an "interlacing, or weaving, or a web," which allows us to disentangle "different threads and different lines of sense or force" so that they can be separated, fused, recombined.[27]

Specifically, deconstruction focuses on the displacement undergone when we privilege the obvious rather than the latent tissues of meaning. We must, argues Miller, be alert to those invisible quotation marks, even within a word, to the margins of texts, to the play of revelation and concealment in language, to the latticework of a text, its contradictions, interweaving, and deceptions."[28] Yet, again, there is a sense in which American deconstruction has focused on the "thereness" of the text in much the same way as did New Criticism. To insist that a text is always already deconstructed, that our teasing and reaping of its tissues is not something we have added to the text but something which constituted it before it was read, is different only in emphasis from Brooks or Warren or Winters. We are accustomed to "recognizing" the autonomy and the inherent ambiguity of a poem; and we are becoming equally accustomed to, and adept at, recognizing that a text can be considered as, to use the current jargon, a figural system closed off from transcendental signification by a grammatological code which gives the text its existence.

But, once again, the American domestication of deconstruction is an emasculation of some of the movement's powerful and exciting challenges to our received notions of "text." Here, I think the potential power of deconstruction for Renaissance scholars can be best realized by posing a series of questions. How can the traditional thematic orientation of Renaissance scholarship deal with the Derridean emphasis, beautifully and elegantly expressed by Hillis Miller on Wordsworth or Hardy, on *différance,* on the infinite deferral of meaning? What do deconstruction's radical views on the emptiness of language have to say about what we assume to be the vitality and plenitude of language in Renaissance texts? In an area of scholarship where "order," "unity," and "decorum" have become shibboleths, what relevance has the deconstructive emphasis on the disruptiveness of textuality? Where seemingly "natural" relations between great originals like Petrarch or Ariosto or Boccaccio and their heirs have valorized terms like "the Petrarchan tradition," what does the deconstructive emphasis on intertextuality and historical dislocation say? Above all, perhaps, where positivist historical scholarship still insists on our need to submit to, say, the Elizabethan World Picture or to become "Shakespeare's contemporary," how can we even start to comprehend the Derridean insistence on the infinitude of reading? In short, when most of the assumptions dominating Renaissance scholarship are so powerful, how can we find a language by which we can talk meaningfully about Renaissance texts and still face the severity of the deconstructive demand? To ask such questions and to attempt to locate such a language are the central tasks in the revival of Renaissance scholarship and, perhaps, literary history generally.[29]

On the surface, deconstruction's concentration on dislocation and disruption conflicts directly with the notions of "unity," "order," and "hierarchy," which are not only, seemingly, part of the philosophical world vision of the Renaissance, but inextricably connected to the very nature of the way historicism approaches the period's texts. Here, of course, historical scholarship sits uneasily alongside the pedagogically seductive ease of New Criticism: indeed, it may be that because lyrics like Marvell's "To His Coy Mistress" or Donne's "The Canonization" seem to lend themselves so easily to New Critical exegesis—the all-you-need-to-know-about-what-this-poem-means-in-fifty-minutes approach—so much Renaissance poetry has been made familiar to undergraduates since the 1940s, and why Spenser remains a specialist's taste and the happy haven of historicist scholars. Where New Criticism, say, locates the text's coherence in its self-contained wholeness, the readings of historicist scholarship have seemingly reinforced such unity by locating it in the philosophical absolutes of the age. I say "seemingly" because I believe that even within an historicist scheme it is amply possible to construct other models of Renaissance intellectual history—as, for instance, a period of surprising upsurges, intellectual dislocations, and above all characteristic *formal* disruptions and silences, especially demonstrable in the literature of the last twenty years of the sixteenth century but, indeed, always incipient in what was after all an extraordinarily insecure age, deserving the title of the "age of anxiety" as surely as our own. Foucault's insistence on the disruptions revealed by the archaeology of a period is a particularly powerful one, especially for a period like the 1590s when so many residual and emergent discourses conflict, intertwine, and dislocate one another.

Deconstruction may therefore, I suggest, become an ally in any attempt to create a new historicist reading of the Renaissance. Yet, of course, it offers more. Along with post-Saussurean linguistics generally, it insists on the text as a palimpsest, "always already inhabited by the track of something that is not itself." Reading reveals textuality as bottomless, its order illusory, its hierarchies arbitrary and repressive. Instead of searching for coherence, we have as our target the *aporias*, what Puttenham termed the figure of "the doubtful," the places or topoi which lead nowhere but further into textuality, revealing not monadic totality but a perpetual play of hidden relations and fragmentariness.[30] For traditional historicist scholars, in our cosy inner rooms, New Critical readings of Donne or Marvell were, it seemed, bad enough, as they revealed (in the convenient institutional structure of seminar or discussion) the multiplicity of verbal meanings (ambiguous or complex) in a text; deconstruction enormously extends their critique by insisting on the infinite polysemy of language and on a ruthless search for the text's heterogeneity.

Deconstruction, then, seems to run directly contrary to our residual historicist methods of reading Renaissance texts. But the radical heterogeneity of reading—the insistence that textual practices operate in contradiction to their own intended existence—might, perhaps, be an exciting way into Renaissance texts. In a period where there seems to have been an enormous pressure upon language to grapple with new experiences, new feelings, new social patterns, language itself is invaded, overflows, struggles. When we read Renaissance texts and sense what Sidney terms their *energeia*, we sense how the production of those texts is only apparently silent, and though a work may attempt to efface the struggle that has produced it, that struggle leaves its invisible but indelible marks. Many of Shakespeare's sonnets, even (perhaps especially) the most serene, derive their energy from providing such a field of struggle. The task of criticism, then, becomes that of bringing to life what has been blotted out, teasing out the discourses that fight within the text. We can watch, for instance in *The Faerie Queene*, how the text maintains an uneasy and shifting relationship with its apparent "philosophical" content, especially through tracing the movements by which it falls short or exceeds what it wants to say (its *vouloir-dire*), and by which it is sidetracked or turned back on itself.[31] We can, most especially, mark the eloquent silences and half-silences, posing the question (the writings of Renaissance women poets like Lady Mary Wroth or Louise Labé, writing within the discursive structures of Petrarchanism, are excellent examples here) of what is a necessary absence, silent or suppressed, in the work.

Interestingly, some Renaissance theorists, notably Sidney, seem to have wrestled with such issues (I confess in passing that just as converted New Critics seem happiest when discussing text, so nostalgic literary historians like myself are happiest when being able to locate precedents in history, a subject to which I will return). We may perceive in Renaissance theory and practice, too, two views of reading—one that sees textuality as communication, a desire to extract conceptual statements from words; the other a desire to escape into the endless play and work of language. In the contrast between Sidney and Greville, for instance, we can see the overflowing productivity of language, its playing off one mode of linguistic organization against another, challenged by a desire to see tropes, meter, and rhyme merely as ornament or as the means for the presentation of ideas. Scholars have long recognized how Ramism, for instance, especially from the 1580s on, tries to force language into the role of a neutral, transparent instrument of an objectified thinking subject, and Greville's Calvinism also attempts to repress what he sensed in Sidney's writing, a promiscuous and anarchic *jouissance* of language, to use Roland Barthes's pregnant term with its suggestion of joy, blïss, and self-forgetting.[32]

In the *Defence,* Sidney seems to hesitate between these two views of language. On the one hand he argues for the primacy and the "reality" of the "fore-conceit" of poetry, yet on the other asserts that the poet never "lieth" or "affirmeth," just as when he discusses the "naming" of characters in drama, he is uneasy about the simultaneous absence and presence of what is signified.[33] What he is fumbling with is the source of authority for poetry. Is it part of rhetoric? Or part of society's aggressive desire to coerce language into meaning? Is a sign always a sign *of?* Or is it in the nature of language always to slip from confined and confining structures of meaning? Does it reproduce a prior reality? Does it reduce that reality to comprehensibility? Or does it free language and with it reading from the coercion of history? In his discussion Sidney brings us within sight of Derrida's warning about the elementary confusion between the literary sign and the object it projects—and it is a confusion that Renaissance poetry articulates as a real anxiety. Greville's battle with the lost origins of words, especially as he wrestles with Sidney's seemingly replete poetry before him, is a compelling example of Geoffrey Hartman's observation that we continually "wish to put ourselves in an unmediated relation to what 'really' is, to know something absolutely."[34] Such a desire is a perpetual anxiety to the Protestant mind, for which the thought that language has powers we cannot control is an invitation not merely to anarchy but to damnation. With enormous struggle, Greville restricts and represses words, overcoming what he clearly perceives as Sidney's promiscuous ebullience of language. Terence Cave's recent account of "writing" in the Renaissance, *The Cornucopian Text,* demonstrates how such a struggle permeated Renaissance thought about poetry. He argues that language was conceived as copious richness, conscious multiplication, and proliferation on the one hand, and on the other, as an instrument in the growth of an authoritarian classicism which had as its aim the control of the multiplicity of language except as a reproducer of the given.[35] So there is Sidney's seeming eagerness to grant full meaning to words in *Astrophil and Stella* and then his constant surprise, or in Greville's case, deep suspicion and fear at finding them determined, limited, or overwhelmed by relations over which they have no control. In so many as yet unexplored ways Renaissance writings triumphantly exemplify how texts belong to language; they illustrate with penetrating clarity how they emerge and are reimmersed in an eternal battle between the imaginary fullness of the world that surrounds them and the tantalizing emptiness of language. A view of Renaissance texts that stresses coherence, unity, closure, avoids the startling perversity of some of the most interesting cultural productions of the period—the obvious formal disunity or dislocaton of major works which claim to be built upon organic wholeness, like *The Faerie Queene,* the *Arcadia, and Measure for Measure.* It is uneasy before radical shifts of tone, changes in authorial stance, stylistic dislocation, shifting personae, and an intense self-reflexiveness, found even in seemingly systematic arguments like Sidney's *Defence.*

In discussing text and textuality, I have already introduced the next and—within the limits of this essay—most unmanageable term, and that is *history.* Most Renaissance scholarship remains committed to a singularly positivistic conception of historicist methodology: to the investigation of diachrony in language, generic form, chronology, causation, and coherent periodization. If we concede, even for the sake of argument, that we cannot maintain that an actual state of the world underwrites the functioning of language, or further, that history itself is available to us only as text, a tissue of fictions and desires, in what sense can we speak of historical scholarship? What is the place of history in the deconstructive model? Or are we—New Criticism is again instructive here—committed to radically ahistorical readings? Is there any final difference between Cleanth Brooks and Jonathan Goldberg?

Once again, I think that if we broaden our perspective on deconstruction itself we can get a more helpful bearing on the deconstructive challenge to literary history. In the past twenty or so years, we have learned (most of us painfully and with puzzlement, especially if we were trained to read in ways we took for granted as "historical") to read literature and write literary history in ways that have little in common with *The Elizabethan World Picture* or *From Donne to Marvell.* Our masters (or goads) have been various: Gramsci and Althusser, Benjamin and Brecht, Foucault, Derrida, Hayden White, Harold Bloom, Hans Georg Gadamer, Hans Robert Jauss, Raymond Williams. Their lessons have been various and their impact puzzling, contradictory, disturbing. But perhaps central to their work is what they share (even when they disagree on most everything else) with deconstruction—a focus on the problematic nature of the confrontation between history and writing, between ideology and textuality.

In the list I have just yoked together is once again the name that above all others is associated with deconstruction—Jacques Derrida. Derrida's own sense of the historicity of reading is almost invariably filtered out by his American disciples—a most revealing misreading of his work. Michael Sprinker has raised the question whether Foucault's reading of Derrida may not have encouraged this narrowing by attacking what he sees as a Derridean pedagogy insisting that there is nothing beyond the text.[36] Yet Derrida can write of "the internal historicity of the work itself" and of "its relationship to a subjective origin that is not simply psychological or mental" and, more surprisingly (if we have learnt to read him through Miller or de Man), of what he terms the determinate force of the author, of intention, and of the productive matrix and historical conditions in the production of meaning. Pressed by the Marxist J. L. Houdebine, Derrida argues for the insufficiency of "a purely formalist criticism which is concerned only with the code, the pure play of the signifier . . . and which neglects the genetic effects or the inscription (historical, if you wish) of the text being read." While he is uneasy about the association of "history" with the linearity, narrative, or presence, he nonetheless praises the "decisive progress" achieved by Althusser, which shows the variety of ways in which different histories may be written.[37] In short, what Derrida, always surprising, thrusts before us is something that the residual New Criticism of American deconstruction has largely ignored—the double determination of language. Language is traversed by conflicting structures of discourse, yes, but also by the formations and systems of representation that define a particular society's culture and ideological life.

Literary texts may, in short, be perceived, not as cultural objects, somehow reflecting or containing a conception of a world, but as practices. We can circumvent the reductionism of an older historicism by the deconstructive insistence on textuality, but the Derridean question loses its power unless we see texts as produced and always in process, within history, in short as *work*, a practice of meaning-production. When deconstruction insists that a text never arrives unaccompanied and that it is engaged in a perpetual struggle to perform the impossible, to represent the real, we can agree and yet still speak of the pressure upon the text of the real, the always absent that is unattainable in language. History is accessible to us only in textual form.[38] The real escapes discourse and can never be made to coincide with language; it is always under erasure and yet nonetheless implicated in the text's struggles. It is our deconstruction of the seeming resolutions of those struggles as we scan the traces of their power of compulsion and repression that allows us access to the conditions of the text's material existence. Texts are haunted by history: in their *aporias,* where they unravel themselves, we locate not the triumphant presence and plenitude of "reality" but the signs of a real struggle which, however effaced, nevertheless pressures and scars them. This is what deconstruction points to and insists we cannot name (just as the text itself may be afraid to)—the struggles it has undergone in history before it emerges in its seemingly homogeneous, unruptured presence.[39]

We read, then, what is being said despite what is apparently said, yes; and reading is an endless process, yes; a text never quite says what it cannot speak, as Macherey puts it.[40] Deconstruction has taught us that it is, indeed, the uncertainties and disruptions in a text, the textual practices that operate to contradict its own intentions, that may speak most powerfully. So we insist on the invisible quotation marks within phrases and words; we attend to the shadowing fault lines where the text deconstructs itself. But even though we cannot assert its presence, we can always note in the systematic absences of the text, at its edges, hidden but eloquent, the power of history and, specifically, the power of ideology. Goldberg, although a little reluctant to move too easily from what he sees as the narcissism of the literary text to the social text, puts it this way: a text, he says, is "responsive to external' systems of meaning" in that it has "already taken them into the text and subjected them to the very narrative structures that determine the action of the poem."[41] Without going beyond or behind the text or establishing ideology as a secret fulcrum, we can assert that each text is a *parole* of a vaster *langue* of ideological discourse. Each text, as Julia Kristeva puts it, belongs to a distinctive ideologeme.[42]

Now I have spelt out, laboriously and at the risk of articulating the obvious, how the text stands as a perpetually renewable reminder of the way words battle within texts, because—it should be clear—I am taking issue with one of the main drives of the American assimilation of deconstruction. To do so, I have introduced a term, ideology, which is suspect from many quarters, one that within the Anglo-American academy can be easily neutralized by being related to a simplistic and crudely reductionist Marxism. But if we take ideology not in the naive sense as a static and even identifiable set of ideas which determines or produces meanings, but as a set of changing and never fully identifiable practices inscribed within language, apparently referential but in fact the encoding of certain lived and therefore changing and volatile relations, then we are able, I believe, to meet and use the full force of the deconstructionist challenge. We can describe ideology as the absence that tantalizes us into accepting presence, a force that structures experience without connoting it. It is not separate from textuality and so somehow "reflected" in texts, but is distributed and inscribed in textuality itself. Its function is the sirenlike interpellation of a text's reader to imagine the self as a unified, central point in the complex and never-ending struggle between author, text, and reader. Ideology tries to bully the text into coherence, to conceal its struggles, to force language to seem to be the transparent and transcendent conveyor of meaning. By dispelling the contradictions that occur between language and its production, ideology attempts to coerce us into privileging and inscribing certain preferred, seemingly natural, meanings over all the other infinite discursive pressures that traverse a text. The role of the critic is, therefore, certainly, to deconstruct, to show up the struggles and strategies, but also to continually reinscribe the text to show how it is a rewriting of prior texts, all of which struggle to imprison it— and by his or her own writing contribute to the work's ongoing history.

The fourth matter of concern to Renaissance scholars is that central concern of much contemporary critical theory and practice, *reading.* Traditional Renaissance scholarship has had a model of the reader submitting himself, usually by detailed contextual studies, to the monumentality of a text and thus showing how a text coheres. The reading is determined by an unproblematic coincidence of authorial intention and a reader's submission. The reader's role, as Harold Bloom nicely mocks, is to be *"responsible* . . . not to revise, correct and reverse, but rather to repeat, congeal and revere."[43] Here, once again, the deconstructive challenge joins forces with an impressive variety of revisionary accounts of reading. It is not only deconstruction which has called into question the search for a single, homogeneous, or at least a limited set of meanings. Reception-aesthetics (Wolfgang Iser), Reader Response Criticism (Stanley Fish, Norman Holland), Reception Semiotics (Umberto Eco), among others, in conflicting but important ways, have constituted what is at the very least a new pedagogy that is fast becoming an orthodoxy in our universities. Indeed, it is fascinating to see how that sternly reproved enemy of New Criticism, the Affective Fallacy, has become widely institutionalized. What deconstruction adds to the increasing orthodoxy of the open-ended nature of texts is both a philosophical skepticism and a rhetorical intensification. Derrida argues that "writing is inaugural," and his remark applies both to intertextuality and to writing's overflowing its apparent boundaries. His assertion that writing "has as its essential objective and indeed takes this fatal risk, the emancipation of meaning"[44] is an insight about some of the most moving critical praxis of recent years. What, in deconstruction's view, enables a text to be read at all and what, by the nature of textuality, infinitely produces new and creative misreadings of texts is what Derrida terms *différance,* the very condition of writing, at once the promise of meaning and the means by which meaning is always deferred. *Différance* is the condition of meaning and the simultaneous guarantee that meaning is impossible, that reading is an endless process, with no central core to arrest the play of the text throughout history. *Différance* at once allows a text to be read and insists that it is unreadable or undecidable, allowing a host of (mis)readings. Finally, there are no texts, only readings (strong or weak) of texts, as meaning disseminates through an endless and inescapable chain of supplementary signifiers: every sign engenders an infinity of new contexts in a manner which is absolutely unlimitable.[45]

There is no doubt that some of the most brilliant criticism of our time—by de Man, Hartman, Bloom—has been deeply influenced by this Derridean emphasis on textual difference and the infinity of dissemination. At once the joy of language and the melancholy reminder of our own mortality, the dissemination of textuality is a disturbing challenge to the philosophical presuppositions of traditional humanist scholarship. Yet it is here, at the absent heart as it were of deconstruction, that the most profound and exciting possibilities for a renewal of historical criticism lie. For finally, once again, the characteristic American reading of Derrida's insights is ideological, invested with the melancholy paralysis of the late twentieth-century Western world. If we speak of there being "finally, no texts, only an infinite textuality always on the move," or of texts as "no longer a finished corpus of writing, some content enclosed in a book or its margins, but a differential network, a fabric of traces referring endlessly to something other than itself, to other differential traces,"[46] then we are speaking of texts decentered, certainly, but we are also speaking of the lives of texts overflowing into history.

Roland Barthes once pointed out, in one of his characteristic brilliant enunciations which once we have read we realize should have been obvious, that most of a work's history comes *after* it is written.[47] If we take Derrida seriously and question the repressive functions of margins, boundaries, signatures, and the referential realm outside the work's frame, then we may perceive the continuity between the text and the textuality that is the work's history—its reading, rereading, translation—which allow us to see the text as part of a network into which our lives and our history are incorporated. Meanings are never produced by texts, or by or within subjects (authors or readers), but between subjects, in networks into which we are written by our class, society, and history. A reading is never outside particular social formations and thus never outside ideology. It does not have a verifiable stability. The work's life as supplementary, as *différance,* allows us to see its history as within textuality and to see deconstruction as allowing us to extend the text into the world, its decentered nature letting it loose into history. A text's readers are subjects in history, inscribed themselves by conflicting languages, cultural as well as literary, not merely the subjects of the text they are reading. We can illustrate this dissemination of textuality very clearly from the history of dramatic works. A play, perhaps more obviously than any other work of art, is always already decentered when it is read, produced, or viewed. There is no original: no original performance, no original "text." A play is a script, decomposing as it is composed, and recomposed as it is performed. It never makes meaning until it is loosed into the world as performance—in short, until it enters the textuality of history. The work initiates performances of meaning, providing us with the signs to read. So we can read the history of, say, Shakespearean criticism as illustrating the changing ways the plays have been read and produced—the shifting fashions (and rewritings) of *Lear,* the obsessive concentration since the early nineteenth century on Hamlet's "inwardness," the changing evaluations of the comedies. Meaning inheres not in the monumental text, but in the necessary and joyfully endless task of interpretation. Meaning is a process of dissemination—it is spilt, spread, always potent.

Readers of Roland Barthes may recall, at this point in the argument, his distinction between "readerly" and "writerly" texts.[48] It is a persuasive and seminal idea. Yet it requires some modification. Any text can be given a writerly reading—and, the deconstructive argument would be, necessarily so. The Renaissance lyric is a case in point. The dynamics of the Petrarchan sequence are such that the originating author is unusually effaced: he offers his poems to a varied audience of sympathetic listeners as a mirror less of his own experiences than of theirs. He becomes one reader among others as he contemplates the experience, listening, reading, "writing," in Barthes's sense. Thus poems within the Petrarchan mode demand dialogue, argument, application. Wyatt's "I wonder what she hath deserved" at the end of "They flee from me" is a question thrust at its audience for completion of its meaning, and the poem inevitably risks an infinitude of possible replies. Sidney's original audiences for *Astrophil and Stella* would have given different, even though to a great extent class-specific, replies to the moral question posed by:

> Let *Virtue* have that Stella's self; yet thus,
> That Virtue but that body grant to us.[49]

While all of Sidney's readers, then and now, share common activities in producing meanings, what they produce will, inevitably and infinitely, be different. The roles for the readers mapped out by the text are not coercive: even within the courtly group among which Sidney wrote, the poems must have variously seduced, tempted, stimulated, pleased, annoyed, even bored. They demanded, and demand, performance, not passivity. Their very life depends on our recognizing that they are loosed, disseminated, in the world.

As in my discussion of author, text, and history, so in my discussion of reading, however simplifying and question-begging at times, I believe we must accept the value, even the indispensability, of the deconstructive challenge—though not necessarily in its characteristic American form. It is instructive, indeed, to glance at Britain, to see how different the assimilation of the Derridean stimulus has been. In those circles in British criticism most open to deconstruction, while Derrida is a name to conjure with, so equally are Lacan and Althusser, Kristeva and Macherey—particularly the last, whose impact on American criticism is minimal and whose impact has been frustratingly (though explicably) neutralized. Indeed, "deconstruction" itself is only one aspect of Derrida's own methodology, and it is a mark of both the poverty of his American disciples and of the imperium of American criticism that until recently the techniques of deconstruction rather than the philosophical concerns of poststructuralism have been identified with Derrida here. Deconstruction is still widely perceived as a mode of interpretation rather than as a wholesale critique of Western metaphysics and cultural history.

For the Renaissance scholar, then, Derrida's remark that the moment of doubling commentary should no doubt have its place in a critical reading,[50] but that criticism must go much further, should be taken as both reassurance and stimulus. It allows us to speak powerfully of the *vouloir-dire* of the text, but to be aware that language's desire is only the edge and never the total expression of the text's experience. It allows us to take the deconstructive question very seriously, but also to speak of the power of texts as they are read and disseminated through their histories and ours.

Wilfrid Laurier University

NOTES

1. Louis Althusser and Etienne Balibar, *Reading Capital*, trans. Ben Brewster (London: Verso, 1970), pp. 15–6. The present paper originated in a Special Session at the 1981 MLA Convention in New York. The author wishes to thank the Research Office of Wilfrid Laurier University for financial support for the research involved.

2. Gerald Graff, "Deconstruction as Dogma, or, Come Back to the Raft Ag'in, Strether Honey!"', *Georgia Review*, 34 (1980), 408.

3. Terry Eagleton, *Walter Benjamin: or Towards a Revolutionary Criticism* (London: Verso, 1981) p. 134; Vincent Leitch, "The Book of Deconstructive Criticism," *Studies in the Literary Imagination* 12 (1979), 19.

4. Michael McCanles, "The Authentic Discourse of the Renaissance," *Diacritics* 10 (March, 1980), 77.

5. See the report on the 1981 Sidney sessions at Kalamazoo, in *Sidney Newsletter*, 1, no.2 (1980), 46.

6. Richard C. McCoy, *Sir Philip Sidney: Rebellion in Arcadia* (New Brunswick: Rutgers University Press, 1980); Stephen Greenblatt, *Renaissance Self-Fashioning: From More to Shakespeare* (Chicago: University of Chicago Press, 1980); Jonathan Goldberg, *Endlesse Worke* (Baltimore: John Hopkins University Press, 1981); William A. Sessions, (ed.), Special Sidney number of *Studies in the Literary Imagination* 15 (1982), especially the essays by Jane Hedley, Annabel Patterson, and Gary F. Waller. For more detailed consideration of Goldberg's important book, see my forthcoming review in *Critical Texts* (1982).

7. Tillottama Rajan, *Dark Interpreter: The Discourse of Romanticism* (Ithaca: Cornell University Press, 1980), p. 16.

8. J. Hillis Miller, "Deconstructing the Deconstructors," *Diacritics* 5 (Summer, 1975), 31.

9. See Geoffrey H. Hartman, *Saving the Text* (Baltimore: Johns Hopkins University Press, 1981), ch. 3; Barbara Johnson, "The Critical Difference," *Diacritics*, 8

(1978), 3; Harold Bloom, "Agon: Revisionism and Critical Personality," *Raritan* 1 (1981), 50.

10. Goldberg, *Endlesse Worke*, pp. xxii. l.

11. Roland Barthes, "The Death of the Author," *Image-Music-Text*, trans. Stephen Heath (London: Fontana, 1977), p. 146; Jacques Derrida, "White Mythology: Metaphor in the Text of Philosophy," *New Literary History*, 6 (1974), 11; Jacques Derrida, *Writing and Differance*, trans Alan Bass (Chicago, University of Chicago Press, 1978), pp. 221–9.

12. Goldberg, *Endlesse Worke*, p. 24.

13. Jonathan Culler, *The Pursuit of Signs* (London: Routledge, Kegan, Paul, 1981), p. 15; cf. Frank Lentriccia, *After the New Criticism* (Chicago: University of Chicago Press, 1980), ch. 5 and J. Hillis Miller, "Deconstructing the Deconstructors," *Diacritics*, 5, no.2 (1975).

14. J. Hillis Miller, "The Critic as Host," *Deconstruction and Criticism* intr. Harold Bloom (New York: Seabury Press, 1979), p. 230. Cf. Miller's remark at the 1981 MLA Convention in New York, that we should abandon the term "deconstruction" since by it we mean, simply, "reading."

15. Bloom, "Agon," 32.

16. Goldberg, *Endlesse Worke*, p. 75.

17. Jacques Derrida, *Of Grammatology*, trans. Gayatri Chakravorty Spivack (Baltimore: Johns Hopkins University Press, 1976), p. 158.

18. Eagleton, *Benjamin*, p. 132.

19. Roland Barthes, *S/Z*, trans. Richard Miller (New York: Hill and Wang, 1974), p. 211.

20. Michel Foucault, *The Order of Things* (New York: Vintage Books, 1970), p. xxiii; Shakespeare, *Coriolanus*, V.iii.36.

21. Roland Barthes, "From Work to Text," in Josué V. Harari, ed., *Textual Strategies: Perspective in Post-Structuralist Criticism* (Ithaca: Cornell University Press, 1970), p. 78.

22. For useful discussions on the positioning of the subject in discourse, see e.g. Catherine Belsey, *Critical Practice* (London: Methuen, 1980), ch. 3; Paul Willemen, "Notes on Subjectivity," *Screen Education* 19 (1978), 41–69; John Brenkman, "Deconstruction and the Social Text," *Social Text* 1 (1979), 186–88.

23. Derrida, *Of Grammatology*, p. 158.

24. Derrida, *Of Grammatology*, pp. 158–519; Edward Said, *Beginnings* (New York: Basic Books, 1975), p. 56.

25. Jonathan Culler, *Structuralist Poetics: Structuralism, Linguistics and the Study of Literature* (Ithaca: Cornell University Press, 1975), p. 30; Harold Bloom, "Agon," 32; see also William E. Cain, "Authors and Authority in Interpretation," *Germanic Review*, 34 (1980), 629–32.

26. Foucault, *The Order of Things*, p. xxiii, "What is an Author?" in Harari, *Textual Strategies*, p. 148. See also William Shullenberger, "Lacan and the Play of Desire in Poetry," *Massachusetts Studies in English* 7 (1978), 33; Diana Adlam and Angie Salfied, "A Matter of Language," *Ideology and Consciousness*, 3 (1978), 95–111. Among recent examples of author-centered Renaissance scholarship might be mentioned A. C. Hamilton, *Sir Philip Sidney: A Study of His Life and Works* (Cambridge: Cambridge University Press, 1977). Hamilton has described his study—which admirably sums up fifty years of twentieth-century scholarship—as an "old fashioned life and works." See the editorial remarks on Hamilton's significance in *Sidney Newsletter* 1, no.2 (1980), 46, and 2, no.1 (1981), 2.

27. Jacques Derrida, *Speech and Phenomena: And Other Essays on Husserl's Theory of Signs*, trans. David B. Allison (Evanston: Northwestern University Press, 1973), p. 132.

28. I hope to elaborate my approach in my forthcoming volume on sixteenth-century poetry in the Longmans History of Literature in English series. At this point, needless to say, my own suggestions are merely playing with the semantic building blocks.

29. Miller, "The Critic as Host," 223.

30. Jacques Derrida, *Writing and Difference*, p. 223; Christopher Norris notes Puttenham's "moralistic" treatment of *Aporia* in *Deconstruction: Theory and Practice* London: Methuen, 1982), p.49.

31. Jacques Derrida, "Positions," *Diacritics* 3,no.1 (1973), 39.

32. Roland Barthes, *The Pleasure of the Text*, trans. Richard Miller (New York: Hill and Wang, 1975), pp. 14, 55, 67.

33. Sir Philip Sidney, *A Defence of Poetry*, in *Miscellaneous Prose of Sir Philip Sidney,*, ed. Katherine Duncan-Jones and Jan van Dorsten (Oxford: Clarendon Press, 1973) pp. 102, 114.

34. Hartman, *Saving the Text*, p. 107.

35. Terence Cave, *The Cornucopian Text* (Cambridge: Cambridge University Press, 1981).

36. Michael Sprinker, "Textual Politics: Foucault and Derrida," *boundary 2*, 8, no.3 (Spring, 1980), 77, 83–4.

37. Jacques Derrida, *Positions*, trans. Alan Bass (Chicago: University of Chicago Press, 1981), pp. 47, 64.

38. Cf. Frederic Jameson, *The Political Unconscious* (Ithaca: Cornell University Press, 1981), p. 35: "history is *not* a text, not a narrative, master or otherwise . . . as an absent cause, it is inaccessible to us except in textual form."

39. For a useful (and still surprisingly neglected) corrective to American deconstruction, which focuses on the text as cultural production, see Pierre Macherey, *A Theory of Literary Production*, trans. Geoffrey Wall (London: Routledge & Kegan Paul, 1978), especially Macherey's emphasis, p. 53, that "a book never arrives unaccompanied: it is a figure against a background of other formations."

40. Macherey, *Literary Production*, pp. 85, 87.

41. Goldberg, *Endlesse Worke*, p. 75.

42. P. N. Medvedev and M. Bakhtin, *The Formal Methhod in Literary Scholarship*, trans. Albert J. Wehrle (Baltimore: Johns Hopkins University Press, 1978), p. 3; Julia Kristeva, "The Bounded Text." *Desire in Language*, trans. Thoman Gora et. al. (New York: Columbia University Press, 1980), p. 36; cf Eagleton, "The Idealism of American Criticism," 6.

43. Harold Bloom, *The Breaking of the Vessels* (Chicago: University of Chicago Press, 1982), p. 28.

44. Derrida, *Writing and Difference*, p. 11.

45. See e.g. Jacques Derrida, "Signature Event Context," *Glyph* 1 (1977), 187; cf Roland Barthes, "Theory of the Text," in *Untying the Text*, ed. Robert Young (Boston: Routledge & Kegan Paul, 1981), p. 42.

46. Jacques Derrida, "Living On," *Deconstruction and Criticism*, pp. 83–84.

47. Barthes, "Theory of the Text," p. 37.

48. Barthes, *S/Z*, pp. 18, 19. Goldberg, p. 12, sees Spenser's *Faerie Queene* as a writerly text. For a reading of Sidney's *Astrophil and Stella* in Barthean terms, see my essay "Acts of Reading: the Production of Meaning in *Astrophil and Stella*," *Studies in the Literary Imagination*, 15 (1982), pp. 23–36.

49. Sir Philip Sidney, "Astrophil and Stella," 52, *The Poems of Sir Philip Sidney,* ed. William A. Ringler, Jr. (Oxford: Clarendon Press, 1962), p. 191.

50. Cf. *Writing and Différance,* p. 32: "When one attempts . . . to pass from an obvious to a latent language, one must first be rigorously sure of the obvious meaning."

The Rhetoric of Consolation: Shakespeare's Couplets

Martha R. Lifson

*M*any of Shakespeare's sonnets 1–126 are concerned with the poet's willed construction of himself, the young man, and their relationship. Like other works of the Renaissance, the sonnets demonstrate a poet's efforts to replace one vivid perception and experience with another. Thus, despite his knowledge of mutability and death, despite his knowledge of mutual betrayal and rot—both growing ironically out of the precious love affair itself—the poet chooses to will a transformation not only of his personal world, but also, by extension, of the world itself.

In moving through the sonnets, the reader encounters powerful descriptions of the loss of love, the mutability of all things, the inevitability of dissolution—the collapse of self in the face of age, death, scandal, jealousy, narcissism, or the powerful ego of another. Sonnet 15, for example, sounds the melancholy note characteristic of the first twelve lines of so many of the poems: "When I consider everything that grows / Holds in perfection but a little moment."[1] Certainly, one of the reasons why the sonnets draw readers in an almost obsessive way is that they focus on such human fears, ones that seem too expansive and awesome to hold in the confines of a formal fourteen-line poem. The sonnets enact a painful human experience of a world or self that seems distined to dissolve just as one gets a momentary fix on it; and they do so not just in one but in many different ways. The themes repeat mercilessly; the stance of the poet-speaker shifts, seemingly firm descriptions are revised; words turn ambiguous or change meaning altogether. The power of language is shown as precarious.

Against this background, the poet makes his bold assertions—

95

that beauty will live on, poetry will survive, love will endure—and
the reader is wrenched abruptly into a very different mood of assurance. It is as if the final two lines are grafted onto the first twelve
in a grand effort to alter the original tendency of the poem: "And,
all in war with Time for love of you / As he takes from you, I
engraft you new" (15). The formal end couplets counter the movement and force of the initial twelve lines and then recede before
their power as the sequence continues on. As one experiences this
movement into the couplet again and again, one is forced to live
through a process of tension among contradictory messages that, I
would argue, becomes as central to a reading of the sonnets as the
themes, images, and subject matter.

The poet's effort appears both hyperbolic and heroic as he dares
to assert the seemingly impossible and to aggrandize those efforts
by showing the reader the very material out of which the new
creation must be wrested. Moreover, the poet emphasizes his
achievement by drawing attention to the fact that all he has to
work with is the often paltry tool of language. He makes us aware
of the work involved by showing us that his only weapons against
dissolution are words as they name, sequence, or fix shifting reality. Sometimes these words attempt to stop time by repeating
pledges of love, as for example in sonnet 76, "For as the sun is daily
new and old, / So is my love still telling what is told." Sometimes
they describe an ideal, as if a kind of mechanical repetitive naming
would make it so:

> Therefore my verse, to constancy confined,
> One thing expressing, leaves out difference.
> Fair, kind, and true, is all my argument
> Fair, kind, and true, varying to other words.   (105)

Here the poet asserts not only the ideal of constancy between two
lovers, but also, by extension, the ideal of constancy as an essence
or principle made viable in the larger world by his verse. More
frequently, the poet creates a metaphor and then treats it as if it
were a reality, showing thereby the power of an inventive mind to
rearrange or gild the world. In sonnet 37 the poet asserts a proposition (let the image of a decrepit father represent the poet, and let
the image of an active child represent the young man), and then
takes comfort in that which he has concocted. Having established
the initial metaphor, the poet goes on to create a metaphor of
abundance, lavishing on the youth beauty, birth, wealth, and wit,

and concludes by describing himself as a sort of parasite, "ingrafting" himself to the abundant store:

> So then I am not lame, poor, nor despised,
> Whilst that this shadow doth such substance give,
> That I in thy abundance am sufficed,
> And by a part of all thy glory live.
> Look what is best, that best I wish in thee.
> This wish I have; then ten times happy me.   (37)

This section of the sonnet makes explicit the role of imagination and language as the poet draws attention to the fact that he has spun the hypothetical plenty from nothing, and yet that he can thereby live on in shared glory.

Yet the poet makes us aware not only of the power of metaphoric language and of words as wishes (possible ways of consoling us in the face of mortality), but also of their frailty, as the whole created fabric unravels, only to be knit up again and again in various attempts to weave it well: he must constantly reassert his belief in truth, poetry, and union in love. The poet is self-conscious, aware of the power and of the limits of his medium and bent on making us also aware. The sonnets draw attention to the poet's efforts to assert what he wants simply by saying it, no matter how contrary it may be to the rest of his experience. What becomes crucial to a reading of the sonnets then is the tension between the first part of the poem, which offers a narrative, and the couplets, which point only to themselves as hyperbolic, rhetorical assertions.[2] (Like other great poems, Shakespeare's sonnets are about the process of creation, and the couplets draw attention to the poet's role as maker, one who wills a certain vision, in the face of common sense or the painful knowledge of chaos, death, and change.) Yet in spite of his efforts, language and the world remain dramatically at odds.

My approach to the sonnets grows, first, out of my dissatisfaction with critical comments which I find, although not unjust, inadequate to my experience of the couplets, and, second, out of critical thought which focuses on reader response, on what the sonnet does as distinct from what it means,[3] and on language and structure as intention.[4] The couplets strike many readers as inadequate and unsatisfactory in the face of overflowing passion and distress. Moreover, since the sonnet is so short a form, the eye cannot help but retrace its path and the ear cannot help but hear echoes of earlier, contradictory lines. All of this has the obvious effect of making the reader edgy and ill at ease. (I would also argue that readers of the sonnets are tantalized because they are unsettled and because they experience the layering of powerful contradictory messages.) It is customary for critics, therefore, to describe the couplets as disjunct from the main body of the sonnets, either weak or tranquil when they continue the same line of argument, or illogical, unconvincing, and merely "poetic" when they take off in a direction counter to the movement of the first twelve lines.[5] That is, the critical effort is to pin down a description of the couplets, rather than to acknowledge either the continuing process back and forth from opening to couplet or the continuing contradictions between "real world" and language, between how a lover might feel and how that same lover turned poet might attempt to address or redress such feelings.

I assume that Shakespeare's sonnets are intentional and dramatic and that the couplets are designed to have the effects they have. It is clear that many readers feel uneasy at the sorts of resolutions which the poet offers: they do not satisfy; they do not resolve in the expected way. Perversely, they do not even clearly fail. Expecting some sort of clear resolution by means of a continuing line of argument or a continuing pattern of imagery, the reader is instead baffled.[6] Thus, the drama of a specific poem is located in the shift from narrative to rhetorical assertion.

In *As You Like It*, Amiens recognizes the ordering power of the poet's mind when he says to the Duke: "Happy is your Grace / That can translate the stubbornness of fortune / Into so quiet and so sweet a style" (II.i.18–20). Even as the Duke's description of Arden is somewhat simplistic and fanciful, so a couplet such as the following may sound simplistic and fanciful: "And all in war with time for love of you, / As he takes from you I ingraft you new" (15). Yet in spite of the assured tone and message of the couplet (in fact, somewhat as a result of it), and because of the weight of the previous twelve lines which introduce the complex theme of mutability, the shift into the couplet is not easy. The drama in sonnets such as this arises from the process, as Amiens calls it, of translation. Since the speakers are knowledgeable and urbane, the reader is forced to recognize and appreciate the effort behind such a remaking of reality, such a willed return to hope and innocence—an effort which as reader I feel as an almost physical wrenching no matter how seemingly solid the end point.[7] And the translation itself is never complete, never stable. The consolation is only in the form of rhetoric, rather than in the form of the beloved's embrace or the radical transformation of the world.

The specific effect of the couplet depends on several factors: on the nature of the statement itself, on the nature of the dramatic tension between the first twelve and the last two lines (how much is being risked), and on the reader's willingness to assent to the couplet (a willingness that may shift even during rereadings of a single sonnet).[8] Although each sonnet must be treated separately, I will attempt to outline some of what I think goes on in a reading. After the initial and powerful lines on mortality, the poet offers a couplet which is rhetorically commanding, usually hyperbolic, and yet unsatisfactory: too brief, bland, pat, illogical, incapable of relieving either the poet's or our own distress. Furthermore, the poet's action seems alternately heroic and self-deluded. I see no clear way to resolve the contradiction nor much gain in their resolution, since the couplet is both audacious and indeed only a couplet, a rhetorical flourish. Art can only do so much to transform life. Nonetheless, in spite of the fact that this couplet cannot obliterate the initial experience of pain, it does provide something consoling and redemptive if only in the poetic images of eternal life or eternal love, if only in the most private arena of memory or wish. Perhaps indeed the sonnets acknowledge and demonstrate that consolation for the pains of love and life can only be private and must always depend on one's own imaginative, lonely endeavors. What one is aware of certainly is the dramatic, rhetorical assertion which provides the important contrary movement to the initial lines. The poet presents weighty evidence and then at the last moment dares the reader to believe a two-line statement, an audacious ploy in spite of the fact that the couplet cuts off further options by authoritatively and formally concluding the poem.[9] It dares to operate like a calm statement of fact: "But if the while I think on thee, dear friend, / All losses are restored and sorrows end" (30).

What one is aware of here is the dramatic operation of the will, much like Edgar's willed redemption of his father in *King Lear*; and since that is so, my assumption is that what we are to attend to is the process of the dramatic and wrenching shift into the couplet and to what it costs, how it fails, how it succeeds, what it demonstrates in terms of human desire, how much is left out of the final solution both in terms of a direct address of specific issues and in terms of human emotion. What is important is not where we have arrived at the end of a reading, but the process itself and the opera-

tion of the "will," particularly given the repeated references to the
word itself; such repetition not only calls attention to the faculty
involved, but is also, as Blackmur asserts, "an obsessive gesture . . .
made out of the single iterated syllable intensified into a half-throt-
tled cry."[10] But the operation of the will, as Nietzsche points out in
Beyond Good and Evil is not simple.[11] In reading the sonnets, one
remains aware of multiple splits, of attention to the first twelve
and to the last two lines, of attention to the poet as both the
commanding and the obeying party (and therefore to the stance of
power by the one, the stance of doubt and reluctance by the other).
Moreover, the grand assertion that appears in the couplet is both
powerful and illusory, the mere appearance of success, both consoling and rhetorical. The reader of the sonnets remains therefore in a
situation psychologically similar to the poet-lover's: in doubt,
urged toward conclusion but ill at ease, aroused (a mirror of erotic
arousal), in suspension. The contradictory evidence of the couplet
functions then as a device for creating doubt, for creating multiple,
mutually contradictory possibilities. Thus the reader experiences
the same desperation as the poet-lover, as the structure of the
sonnet mirrors the love affair; both must acknowledge that rhetoric and poetry are never enough in the face of mortality and yet
that they must serve, even grandly.

I will address three conventional groups of sonnets, specifically
those which critics have singled out as failing at the end: poems on
constancy, poems on union, and poems on time, concluding with a
discussion of sonnet 116.

Poems on Constancy

The specific image of constancy in love is difficult for the poet to
establish and sustain both in the body of the poem and especially
in the couplets. (Of course, since the reader has no other
knowledge about the youth, the poet creates not only the image of
constancy, but also the previous one of inconstancy.) Sonnet 53
asks the young man, "What is your substance," and continues:

> Describe Adonis, and the counterfeit
> Is poorly imitated after you;
> On Helen's cheek all art of beauty set,
> And you in Grecian tires are painted new.
> Speak of the spring and foison of the year;
> The one doth shadow of your beauty show,

The other as your bounty doth appear,
And you in every blessed shape we know.
In all external grace you have some part,
But you like none, none you, for constant heart.

The final line lands hard on "constant heart"—in part because of
the end rhyme, in part because it sounds definite after the fumbling, repetitious, "but you like none, none you," and in part because the phrase appears to be the end point of an argument which
is never made. In fact, the poet's description of the young man as
constant is in opposition to the earlier comparison of the youth
and Adonis (distant and rejecting in *Venus and Adonis*) or the
youth and Helen (one cannot help but recall that she is mythically
inconstant, although it is her beautiful cheek alone which is in-
voked). Thus as readers we are forced to pay attention to a phrase
that in the context of Adonis and Helen as cheats, rather than or as
well as beautiful, can only seem inappropriate, if not embarrassing.
The reader meanwhile is set in multiple directions at once: the
poet has brought off a grand and benevolent gesture; the poet is
trying to embarrass the young man into constancy; the poet pro-
tests too much and in too hyperbolic a fashion, and therefore
causes us to judge the young man even more harshly; the poet has
placed a verbal label on the youth almost like a slap, a rebuke for
the discrepancy between label and fact—it will never stick.[12] Since
the poem begins with a question, "What is your substance, wherof
are you made," the final line sounds like a sort of answer, willed,
assertive, subject to doubt, but better than no attempt at all. The
poet attempts to make the boy in the image he wants, to replace
the older literary figures of Helen and Adonis with his own. This
poem and others on constancy demand also a remaking of the
poet-lover himself who must set aside one way of being for
another, who must turn away from himself as jealous, abject lover,
and become instead grand pronouncing poet. The "boy" longing for
love (even taking some pleasure in being disgraced) must become
the father of decree. Such reconstruction, such consolation—especially as it is private and rhetorical—remains uneasy, but also poignant, abjectly grand, as if the poet would straddle both poles.

Sonnet 54 operates in a similar way, ending with, "And so of
you, beauteous and lovely youth, / When that shall fade, my verse
distills your truth," although the poem has in no way established a
connection between the young man and truth, in fact has done
quite the opposite. This poem makes even more manifest than the

preceding one what power it is that makes and distills "your truth": "my verse." The poet is as much aware of naming as a transforming power as he is of love. Although many poems describe love and its effect (e.g., sonnet 57), it seems to me that it is not, as critics have suggested, the power of love that convinces the reader, but rather the assertive words themselves. Love may falter, as it often does in the poems, but the image of it carried by the imagination and words does not. Obviously the poet remains ambivalent toward the young man in the sonnets, in spite of his verbal assertions. Sometimes he will use a verbal device, such as repetition, which seems to put an end to all difficulty, to lock their love in place, but which also undercuts it—as when "my love" in sonnet 40 seems to refer to the poet's affection, to the young man, and perhaps even to the mistress. Such playing with words can carry the potential of liberation and joy, a way out of a locked situation or a sense of injury, but here, it seems to me, the return to the phrase "my love" is obsessional, ironic, and pained:

> Take all my loves, my love, yea, take them all:
> What hast thou then more than thou hadst before?

Moreover, the couplet to sonnet 40 employs several expressions which carry multiple meanings and which can therfore produce uneasiness in the reader:

> Lascivious grace, in whom all ill well shows,
> Kill me with spites; yet we must not be foes.

"Well shows" could mean either that error which shows in an obvious and reprehensible way—thus picking up an ehco from "lascivious"—or that even error looks beautiful in the young man, thus emphasizing "grace," which itself carries the double sense of graceful and blessed. In this poem, as in most concerning the youth's constancy, the context of the rest of the sequence alters our sense of the sonnet's meaning and tone; it is therefore difficult to accede completely to whatever argument or posture the poet adopts, since elsewhere he may embrace its opposite and reveal the contradictory and illusory nature of our only source of information.[13]

Sonnet 34 also concerns constant love as it is seemingly promised by the young man, as it is subsequently betrayed and finally as it is recreated in the couplet:

> Why didst thou promise such a beauteous day
> And make me travel forth without my cloak,
> To let base clouds o'ertake me in my way,
> Hiding thy brav'ry in their rotten smoke?
> 'Tis not enough that through the cloud thou break
> To dry the rain on my storm-beaten face,
> For no man well of such a salve can speak
> That heals the wound, and cures not the disgrace:
> Nor can thy shame give physic to my grief;
> Though thou repent, yet I have still the loss:
> Th' offender's sorrow lends but weak relief
> To him that bears the strong offense's cross
> Ah, but those tears are pearl which thy love sheeds,
> And they are rich, and ransom all ill-deeds.

Hilton Landry finds this couplet suspiciously abrupt annd con-cludes that "one may doubt that an excess of loving forgiveness has actually overcome the justifiably strong resentment displayed in the quatrains."[14] Murray Krieger declares: "Finally this meta-phor works the trick, if only by fiat. The 'Ah' suggests the sudden, surprising discovery of the specious opening that the metaphor in the couplet offers him. The poet leaps to grasp the unearned trans-fer from 'tears' to 'pearl' to 'ransom' which appears to solve the problem only at an unsubstantive level of language."[15]

What fascinates me is exactly what bothers these critics, that is, the poet's often faltering and dramatic efforts to defy loss and be-trayal with two lines of verse. Since Shakespeare's couplet makes no logical sense and certainly cannot offset the weight of the ear-lier part of the poem, the only way a reader can believe or assent to it is as a willed assertion on the part of the speaker against the young man's behavior and against his own resentment.[16] It may also be that the poet consciously embraces the role of holy fool, showing that he is quite willing to love beyond reason, beyond logic. More importantly, however, he decrees a new reality on top of an already established and even hyperbolic image of pain in which he dares to describe himself as bearing "strong offense's cross." It seems to me that the sonnets demonstrate not the unsub-stantive level of language, though language is questioned at every turn, but rather the power of language. Although the poet is obvi-ously unable to control the experience he describes, nevertheless as poet he has supreme and total control over language which proffers resolution, even redemption.

It is clever manipulation of words that allows the poet to turn storm "rain" to "tears" to "pearl," to transform the shape and meaning of the other, and it is sheer audacious rhetoric that allows the poet to console himself with the rich and substantial pearls which he has just created of watery, transitory tears. We are not unaware of the haunting echoes of the earlier lines, of the pain and grief of the speaker, but I would argue that the effect of the whole poem, including these earlier echoes, is complex, and that we cannot avoid the position in which we are placed by describing the couplets as either completely calm and satisfactory or as completely fake and unearned. Rather, I think we must bear the difficulty of remaining in the same state as the poet—a bit uneasy and willfully holding onto the rhetoric lest we slip back into the body of the poem.[17]

Sonnet 33 also presents the problem of holding onto the couplet as the poet asserts that the young man is not to be rejected for his wanton behavior: "Yet him for this my love no whit disdaineth; / Suns of the world may stain when heav'n's sun staineth." In reading this, one is forced to try to hold back the reverberations of the early parts of the argued metaphor in which the poet censures his love as one who permits his own disgrace (allowing "The basest cloud to ride / With ugly rack on his celestial face") lest such censure undermine the rhetoric of the conclusion. Such holding action is necessary for the poet in creating a figure he can love, but it is also a strain, one in which the reader too participates.

Sonnet 56 provides another instance in which the poet chooses rhetoric as consolation, here for the fading of love's force. Moreover, here he also makes explicit his use of literary devices, hyperbole and metaphor, by drawing attention to a poet's arbitrary powers. At first he piles metaphor upon metaphor in order to transform dullness into passion:

> Sweet love, renew thy force; be it not said
> Thy edge should blunter be than appetite,
> Which but today by feeding is allayed,
> Tomorrow sharp'ned in his former might.

In the couplet, however, the poet shifts tactics; for although he finally faces the pain of diminution by employing the metaphor of winter, he immediately brushes that aside to look to a future embrace of passion appropriately compared to summer: "As *call it* winter, which, being full of care, / Makes summer's welcome, thrice *more wished,* more rare" (my emphasis). We see the poet self-consciously choosing the metaphors in order to effect what he wants, in order to establish the inevitable arrival of summer which as the seasons go always follows winter.

In sonnet 109 the poet assumes his role of commanding poet even more completely, if also ironically, as he names the young man "my rose" and "my all," and in so doing not only transforms the young man to "all," but the rest of the universe to "nothing":[18]

> Never believe, though in my nature reigned,
> All frailties that besiege all kinds of blood,
> That it could so preposterously be stained
> To leave for nothing all thy sum of good—
> For nothing this wide universe I call
> Save thou, my rose; in it thou art my all.

What becomes of interest then is the functioning of rhetoric,[19] and the poet's audacious and self-conscious use of it, (reflected in his language of arduous belief, choice, naming, and even striving: "You are my all the world, and I must strive / To know my shames and praises from your tongue," 112), and its operations on the reader, who experiences a shifting state of affairs within the poems and a changing willingness to assent to the various transformations effected.

Poems on Union

In order to create and maintain an image of the young man's virtue and constancy, the poet even undertakes to remake himself, identifying with the young man's point of view or even with the young man in his entirety, as in the couplets to sonnets 62 and 25:

> 'Tis thee, myself, that for myself I praise,
> Painting my age with beauty of thy days.
> Then happy I that love and am beloved
> Where I may not remove, nor be removed.[20]

In this second example, the poet wills the two into faithful union and pronounces himself therefore "happy" (cf. also sonnet 92),[21] a word which might appear simplistic were it not for the consciousness of what has gone before. In the series of sonnets 87–93, in

which the poet fears the loss of his friend's love, the poet frequently proposes to abandon his own identity in order to maintain
his love, and whatever struggle may be exhibited in the sonnet
proper is resolved in the couplet by the rhetorical maneuver of
calling two, one. Having posited a center for his poems and for the
universe, he refuses to acknowledge that the center may be fickle
or without value, despite the evidence—one result of which would
be the obliteration of all that he is as poet. Rather, the poet portrays himself as worthless, self-consciously choosing self-deception
and abandonment of self in order to maintain his vision. He makes
himself so much a part of the youth that in robbing himself he
paradoxically gains:

> The injuries that to myself I do,
> Doing thee vantage, double vantage me.
> Such is my love—to thee I so belong—
> That for thy right myself will bear all wrong.   (88)

In sonnet 89 the poet uses all his poetic powers to create an image
of himself as powerless, and again the reason behind his maneuvers
seems to be that his will is elsewhere and that he must form
himself anew even to the point of embracing disgrace and denial of
self:

> For thee, against myself I'll vow debate,
> For I must ne'er love him whom thou dost hate.

(A bit perversely perhaps one might argue that for a poet all sense
of reality must be reduced to one—one imagination, one universe,
one creator; the sonnets poignantly demonstrate that it is indeed
the poet who is more in the wrong because more dedicated to the
singular and to a union in which one or the other must be obliter-
ated.) In this context the speaker appears to us both as weak, in his
role as a lover willing to abandon his sense of self, and as potent, a
poet supremely able to alter reality to accord with his sense of how
it ought to be.

Sonnet 37 also points up the speaker's dual role since he is at one
time both the lover wronged, a lover willing to remake himself
(delude himself), and the poet, able to make up the world if necessary: "Look what is best, that best I wish in thee. / This wish I
have, then ten times happy me." Because of the speaker's double
role, this ending can be heard in two ways: (1) as a rather hysterical

and desperate wish by a man who will remain lame, poor, and despised no matter how much he identifies with the young man's plentitude, and (2) as an act of tremendous imaginative will, a statement of absolute certitude that draws attention to the poet as maker and creator.[22]

Sonnet 71 also makes the two men one, but here by drawing the young man into the poet's sphere, as the poet wishfully identifies him with his own perceptions and self-pity. Here the poet projects himself forward in time. Posturing for effect, he constructs himself in a certain way in order to draw pity from the young man:

> No longer mourn for me when I am dead
> Than you shall hear the surly sullen bell
> Give warning to the world that I am fled
> From this vile world, with vilest worms to dwell.

Although the poet urges the young man to forget him as soon as he is dead, the effect of his insistence on his worthlessness, on his imminent death, and on probable neglect is to draw attention to his extreme selflessness and thus to his need for reciprocal love. The couplet to sonnet 73 states exactly what end the poet has in mind: "This thou perceiv'st, which makes thy love more strong, / To love that well which thou must leave ere long." The effect of this couplet on the reader, however, is far from simple, although like many other couplets it could be described as in itself a simple, straightforward statement. What happens is that the reader is unsettled by this conclusion and is forced to wonder about the transition: why does the couplet sound so assured (though even here, I would admit, the negative implications of the last words somewhat color that certainty) when the rest of the sonnet is frantic, uncertain, and filled with shifting images and rhythms? Thus the effect of the transition is to make the reader experience the couplet as something other than a neat conclusion. Furthermore, the couplet forces us to ask who really perceives what the sonnet describes. It is obvious that it is the poet—at least initially—who knows how he feels and who projects a particular image of himself, and that the couplet, without cause, both identifies the young man's perception with his own and posits an effect of that perception—stronger love. Since, however, the reader has no reason to believe that the young man sees the poet's decay, nor that he loves him more (in part because the process has been constructed within the solipsistic confines of the sonnet itself, and in part because the young man has no voice of his own), the positive assertion in the couplet acts on the reader as pure invention, an exhilarating and unsettling act of will.[23]

Poems on Time

The sort of shift from the body of the poem to the couplets which I have been discussing is very clear in the sonnets about time in which the couplets announce that the youth will live eternally in the poet's verse, but in which the earlier lines portray death unforgettably and graphically as carving, delving, devouring, and laying siege. Sonnet 19 presents two types of poetic fiat. Before the couplet, the poet decrees: "But I forbid thee one most heinous crime, / O carve not with thy hours my love's fair brow, / Nor draw no lines there with thine antique pen." The expletive, the repeated negatives, the vivid imagery, and the first person direct address to death make this a powerful statement. The couplet, however, takes a new tack, acknowledging the poet's inability to stop time and asserting a new reality: "Yet do thy worst, old time; despite thy wrong, / My love shall in my verse ever live young." Although the couplet makes a different argument, allowing first the falling rhythm of failure, as time destroys the youth, it nonetheless shows the poet in the same stance: setting creative will against the destructive powers of mortality. Furthermore, although the couplet has been described as weak, it is not. The poet does, however, risk the possibility of the couplet's failure by using such plain, simple words; and he risks his own stature by self-consciously embracing so obvious a burden of turning words to truth:

> Yet do thy worst, old time; despite thy wrong,
> My love shall in my verse ever live young.

In sonnet 123 the poet consciously defies time, vowing and willing to be ever true to his love:

> This I do vow, and this shall ever be,
> I will be true despite thy scythe and thee.

Sonnet 65 hopes that the miracle of verse will allow the young man to live forever, and sonnet 107, while vividly presenting the power of time to change all things, ends by asserting the eternal monument of poetry:

> And thou in this shalt find thy monument,
> When tyrants' crests and tombs of brass are spent.

This poem extends the poet's hyperbolic attitude even further, since he not only creates a monument out of the small form at hand, but even asserts his own eternity, and vows that in spite of Death's power, "I'll live in this poor rhyme."

In any number of similar poems then, the poet self-consciously moves from an awareness of change, fragmentation, and decay to an assertion of power; or from the ironic mode which encompasses loss, fragmentation, separation (spacially and temporally as well as ontologically) to the hyperbolic and unifying: I am happy and rich / we are one / you and I live eternally.[24] As a result the reader is aware both of the poet's efforts to transform events and of the residue left by the first twelve lines even when he apears to succeed. We cannot help but be aware of the considerable rhetorical and dramatic effort necessary to change time into eternity, verse into life itself. Committed to the word, the poet's effort is not unlike the effort of faith itself, and as in reading the poems of Donne, we are moved not so much by a final statement as by the struggle, the creative effort.

I will conclude with a brief discussion of sonnet 116, an interesting and complex sonnet for many reasons: because it seems to refer to so many other sonnets on various subjects, because no matter how a given statement initially appears, it must somehow be modified or adjusted, because it defies explication, and because it is so clearly rhetorical. The poem opens with what appears to be a straightforward assertion of human will against the process of change or imperfection. The poet instructs himself to continue in his creation of love as he will have it:

> Let me not to the marriage of true minds
> Admit impediments. Love is not love
> Which alters when it alteration finds,
> Or bends with the remover to remove.

Yet, since the lines reveal the poet's awareness that love may change, the assertion seems self-consciously determined, hyperbolic, rhetorical. The poet will not "admit impediments," that is, will not allow faults access to his definition, will not even confess that a word such as "impediments" might exist.

The whole poem is filled with strong definitions of love—"love is not," "it is an ever-fixed mark," "it is the star," "love's not time's fool," "love alters not"—some of which, again by including the negative, reveal the enormous effort necessary to instill its opposite. As in the other sonnets I have discussed, it is as if the poet acknowledges a reality—change, mutability, falsehood, betrayal—only to embrace another reality and to make love what he wants and needs it to be by means of language. Thus the reader has the experience of overlay, of one truth laid on top of, but never obliterating another truth beneath.[25] The reader is aware not so much of the poet's lack of logic (although critics have faulted him for this), nor of the strength of his love, but rather of his endeavors to transform, of his personal poetic powers. He stakes everything on his having "writ," sees everything from his chosen perspective as poet:

> Love's not time's fool, though rosey lips and cheeks
> Within his bending sickle's compass come.
> Love alters not with his brief hours and weeks,
> But bears it out ev'n to the edge of doom.
>   If this be error, and upon me proved,
>   I never writ, nor no man ever loved.

In the couplet, which continues with a complex overlay of information,[26] the poet acknowledges the possibility that the whole assertion about the marriage of minds could be error, could, in fact, be proved false. Yet he says he stakes his belief on love and his writing, both of which are able to transform the world. Since the sonnet sequence witnesses that he has written and loved, the logical conclusion would be that his final assertion is true; moreover, the poet quite obviously draws us as readers into his rhetorical and heroic stance against time by referring to love as it has existed in the world, as all of us have participated in it. Yet since the couplet is stated conditionally, as well as hyperbolically, the reader also experiences it as somewhat shaky. It is as if the poet both questions and, given the fact that he is in the midst of his words and work, embraces his role and its transforming powers. On the one hand, the poem appears more assured than many of the others since the poet creates the illusion of speaking aloud (cf. the reference to the marriage ceremony) both to the young man and to a larger, more general audience, and since he is so self-conscious about his role and its power to validate his assertions. On the other hand, the poet never frees his readers from uncertainty and thus makes us conscious of the difficulty with which he proclaims his final words and of the wrenching that is necessary to move from the possibility of error to the power of the word. He lets us know what it costs to construct a reality of assertion, and as a reader, I feel exhilarated by having him placed under such tension and strain by this couplet and by many of the rest. As readers of Shakespeare's sonnets, we see more than the reestablishment of order or the pallid hopes for love; we participate in poetry as a miraculous condition or enactment of the will.

Occidental College

NOTES

1. Except where noted, my quotations are from *Shakeseare's Sonnets,* ed. Stephen Booth (New Haven: Yale University Press, 1977). I have also used the Pelican edition of the *Sonnets,* ed. Douglas Bush and Alfred Harbage (Baltimore: Penuin Books, 1961). Sonnet numbers are given in the text.

2. Murray Krieger, *A Window to Criticism* (Princeton: Princeton University Press, 1964).

3. See Stanley Fish, "Literature in the Reader: Affective Stylistics," in *Self-Consuming Artifacts* (Berkeley and Los Angeles: University of California Press, 1973), pp. 383–487.

4. See, for example, Paul de Man, "Form and Intent in American Criticism," in *Blindness and Insight* (New York: Oxford University Press, 1971), or Joseph Riddel, *The Inverted Bell* (Baton Rouge: Louisiana State University Press, 1974).

5. Philip Martin, for example, in discussing sonnet 62, remarks, "the couplet does, I think, feel a bit glib, and on its own it lacks the resources needed to give enough imaginative force to the idea that the beloved is a second self" (*Shakespeare's Sonnets* [Cambridge: Cambridge University Press, 1972,] p. 48). Concerning sonnet 30, Martin is in accord with M. M. Mahood and G. Wilson Knight in finding the couplet perfunctory and trite, p. 105. In reference to the same sonnet, Edward Hubler says that the couplet, unlike those in similar sonnets introducing an antithetical point of view, is saved from emphasis by the relaxed lines which lead up to it. "But generally Shakespeare's failures with the couplet are owing to a danger inherent in the sonnet form which he chose and to his impatience with formal problems" (*The Sense of Shakespeare's Sonnets.* [Princeton: Princeton University Press, 1952], p. 27). In trying to justify this couplet, Stephen Booth perhaps also unwittingly damns it by arguing that the lines release a reader from intellectual involvement in the poem, assuring him that "after all he has only been reading a poem" (*An Essay on Shakespeare's Sonnets* [New Haven: Yale University Press, 1969], p. 143). In his introduction to the Signet edition, W. H. Auden remarks that the "couplet lines are the weakest and dullest in the sonnet, and, coming where they do at the end, the reader has the sense of a disappointing anticlimax" (*Sonnets,*

ed. William Burto [New York: NAL, 1964], p. xxv]. None of these critics considers an idea suggested to me by Murray Krieger that sonnet 31 tries to earn metaphorically what seems to be gratuitous in sonnet 30. My only difficulty with this is that a reader is still stuck with the peculiar impact at the end of the single sonnet. If sonnet 31 can modify one's response, I do not find that it can obliterate it.

6. See Wolfgang Iser, "The Reading Process: A Phenomenological Approach," in *The Implied Reader* (Baltimore: The Johns Hopkins University Press, 1978).

7. Anton Prikhofer describes the poet as assuming the stance of a playwright when he wills a particular point of view. "The Beauty of Truth," in *New Essays on Shakespeare's Sonnets,* ed. Hilton Landry (New York: AMS Press, 1976), p. 127.

8. See Norman Holland, *Poems in Persons* (New York: Norton, 1973).

9. Barbara Herrnstein Smith, *Poetic Closure* (Chicago: University of Chicago Press, 1968), pp. 182–86. Hyperbole "can have the same sort of dramatic or contextual validity that we observed earlier in connection with the 'illogical' conclusions of pseudo-logical poems, and may have closural force for similar reasons. They are experienced with reference to the speaker's motives, feelings, and circumstances; and, as we know from non-literary situations, a speaker's desire or willingness to make hyperbolic statements" (p. 185).

10. R. P. Blackmur, *Language as Gesture* (New York: Harcourt, Brace, 1952), p. 13. Referring to the repetition of "will," Blackmur states: "It is not at all the meaning the words *had* that counts, but the meaning that repetition, in a given situation, makes them take on"?

11. Friedrich Nietzsche, *Beyond Good and Evil,* trans. Walter Kaufmann (New York: Vintage Books, 1966) pp. 25–27.

12. Hilton Landry comments that when the hyperbolic assertion in sonnet 53 is examined in the light of sonnets 48, 49, 52, 54, and 56, "one must conclude that it probably springs less from an attitude of confident assurance than from one of fearful hope." *Interpretations in Shakespeare's Sonnets* (Berkeley and Los Angeles: University of California Press, 1963), p. 50.

13. Booth's edition prints "by," the Q reading, rather than "my," but I have preferred "my." Like sonnet 54, 57 is also full of contradictions, among which are: (1) I think no ill of you / I am a fool for not finding fault in what pains me; (2) I think no ill of you / I am jealous; (3) I have nothing to do but wait on you, wait for you / I resent this waiting and I resent being a slave (the interrogative form questions the statement: "Being your slave, what should I do but tend / Upon the hours and times of your desire?"); (4) I do not mind waiting for you / I hate waiting and time drags—I describe time as the "world-without-end hour"; (5) I think only of how happy your friends are who are with you / I can think only of how sad, jealous, weary I am.

Occasionally the poet sets up an expectation only to frustrate it and thereby to contribute to the ambiguous nature of his stance; or he uses phrases which carry several expectations. The phrase "knowledge of mine own desert" in sonnet 49 might lead us to expect (1) anger directed toward the young man who seemingly searches out reasons to reject the poet, or (2) an attack on himself since he has no worth. Although this second expectation is the one realized in the poem, the reader yet feels the harshness if not the unjustness of the rejection.

G. Wilson Knight discusses the power of the poet's thought-self in sonnets 44, 50, 51 to obliterate space, thus uniting him with his absent friend. *The Mutual Flame* (London: Methuen, 1955), pp. 46–47.

14. Landry, *Interpretations,* p. 59.

15. *Window to Criticism*, p. 156. In his note to sonnet 34, 11, 13–14, Booth states that the presence in the couplet of the same elements that composed its twelve-line opponent asserts an extralogical justice to the couplet.

16. Landry, *Interpretations*, p. 53; Krieger, *Window to Criticism*, p. 156.

17. Renaissance poetry often presents this difficulty for the reader, of having to hold onto a perspective quite willfully lest one slip into another; I think, for example, of the difficulty of holding onto one meaning of the word "wanton" to describe Eve's free and unbound locks of hair lest one slip into an easier perspective and comdemn her as already fallen before she actually falls in Book IX of *Paradise Lost*.

18. Because Shakespeare himself refers to alchemy in his sonnets, it is tempting to use the metaphor to explain the process at work in the poems. G. Wilson Knight draws attention to Shakespeare's use of the imagery of gold: "Can we say that 'love' transmuting, like 'alchemy' base things to gold, has given him an insight into the truth of creation?" *The Mutual Flame*, p. 121.

19. Booth, *Shakespeare's Sonnets*, p. 353: "The hyperbolic compliment in lines 13 and 14 depends on reversing the common sense judgment that the universe—the sum, the whole—is greater than any one of its constituent parts in worth as well as in bulk." Cf. also Winifred Nowottny, "Some Features of Form and Style in Sonnets 97–126," *New Essays on Shakespeare's Sonnets*, ed. Hilton Landry, p. 103.

20. It may be useful to analyze the sonnets as well in terms of tropes; in general the first twelve lines proceed by way of metaphor and metonymy, and the couplet, as I have indicated, by hyperbole. For example, sonnet 25 compares the young man to a prince who is then compared to the sun; the poet becomes a favorite, a court, and then a flower turning its face to the sun. The line "Great princes' favorites their fair leaves spread" employs metonymy in "leaves"; it is also anticipatory since the marigold does not appear until the next line, and a bit ironic since the other sonnets establish that the young man does not treat the poet as a favorite. Within the young man-prince metaphor, the prince then frowns (metonymy) and "kills" those whose pride is buried ("And in themselves their pride lies buried"). The couplet finally is illogical and hyperbolic: "Then happy I, that love and am beloved / Where I may not remove nor be removed" (cf. sonnet 116). The former relationship between the poet and the young man was that of contiguity; in the couplet, the relationship is one of merging and unity. Speaking of hyperbole in "The Map of Misprision" Harold Bloom relates this trope (metalepsis or metonymic hyperbole) to a "representation set against time, sacrificing the present to an idealized past or hoped-for future." *Map of Misreading* (New York: Oxford University Press, 1975), p. 103.

21. In discussing sonnet 92, Leishman draws particular attention to the poet's willed exaltation of the self, an observation with which I am in obvious agreement. J. B. Leishman, *Themes and Variations in Shakespeare's Sonnets* (London: Hutchinson, 1963), p. 212.

22. Often this process seems similar to the process which Milton describes in the prologues to *Paradise Lost*. Envisioning himself as chaos—dark, unformed, unredeemed—he then works his way toward creation and the light (see, for example, III, 51–55). Although Shakespeare's is often a reverse process, i.e., denying himself by taking on the wrongs and faults of another, the effort and risk is the same, and frequently also the tone of voice: "so be it."

23. A useful context for sonnets 71–74 is *Astrophel and Stella*, for in these sonnets Shakespeare parallels Sidney not only by self-consciously constructing an image of himself, but more importantly by using the couplet to assert a new reality

in place of the old. Also, by means of an artificial creation, Astrophel, Sidney is able to meditate about his own feelings, especially about his own identity. Furthermore, this character, in spite of his protestations of sincerity and artlessness, makes a deliberate posture, knows he is doing so, and finds all of the antics of love interesting because they show the many facets of himself (cf. 45, 33, 10). In *An Apology for Poetry*, Sidney outlines the method which both poets seem to follow. First praising the poet for improving upon nature, for making a golden world, he goes on to say that the poet creates a lover more true than any real lover could be. Interestingly, both the sonnet and the pastoral, as highly artificial modes, recognize that it is the mind that makes good or ill, and both value the power of mind that can produce the image of the graces on Mt. Acidale or Shakespeare's image of love.

24. Or as Paul de Man might say, from the ironic to the allegorical. "The Rhetoric of Temporality," in *Interpretations, Theory, and Practice*, ed. Charles Singleton (Baltimore: The Johns Hopkins Press, 1969). This article has influenced my thinking throughout as well as the actual title of this essay.

25. See Booth, *Essay*, p. 175.

26. Booth, *Shakespeare's Sonnets*, p. 389. Also Booth, *Essay:* "By means of the analyses that follow, I hope to suggest that the couplets, even those as apparently debilitating as the grand hollow couplet of 116, serve a purpose similar to the speeches of political reestablishment at the ends of *Hamlet* and *Macbeth*. The tragedies put their audiences' minds through a turmoil of conflicting systems of value. Fortinbras and Malcolm return order to the stage; they do not resolve the conflicts in the mind of the onlooker, but they do reestablish order in one of the threatened systems. The completion of the story, the completion of the artistic whole, and the resolution of the *particular* conflict of the play puts a frame to the audience's experience of intellectual turmoil and makes it bearable" (p. 131).

Anger, Wounds, and the Forms of Theater in *King Richard II:* Notes for a Psychoanalytic Interpretation

Murray M. Schwartz

For C. L. Barber

King Richard II stages two versions of kingship, each a double of the other and divided in itself. In each we experience versions of theater, envolving relations between action and the self-consciousness of action. Moreover, these versions of theater bespeak different relations between symbolic display and the politics of power. I am interested in the kinds and modes of enactment Shakespeare used, tested, or inhibited in the play, and, most importantly, in achieving a psychoanalytic understanding of the relations between the play's varieties of theatrical experience and what we might call the "deep structures" of Shakespeare's imagination revealed most fully in the astonishingly complex resonance of his language. For even in the theater, where the realities of staging inform our responses to Shakespeare's linguistic possibilities, we still each undergo a complex experience mediated by the web of language.

Psychoanalytic interpretation seeks to infer connections between language and action that point to the reenactment of unconscious analogues informing the work, not in order to reduce the work to those analogues, but to show their transformed significance in a social space. These notes are meant to suggest how some forms of theater can be illuminated by psychoanalytic speculations related to them by a common quest for representation of identity in time.

115

In act V, scene ii, York voices the association between the power of politics and the power of theater:

> As in a theatre the eyes of men,
> After a well-grac'd actor leaves the stage,
> Are idly bent on him that enters next,
> Thinking his prattle to be tedious;
> Even so, or with much more contempt, men's eyes
> Did scowl on Richard.   (23–28)[1]

At this moment, Shakespeare is using his theater to reflect the historical transformation of the political arena into a theatrical space. Bolingbroke's visual presence, "Mounted upon a hot and fiery steed" (8) feeds the "greedy looks of young and old" (13), making the urban world a stage, and the Shakespearean stage a verbal re-creation of a seductive image of power. A simple simile on one level, this recriprocal mirroring of the historical world and the theater required the kind of social and psychological transformation that the action of *Richard II* dramatizes. By inviting us to imagine the king from the position of a theater audience, Shakespeare is responding to an actual historical crisis. He created *Richard II* at a time when this crisis could be felt acutely as it affected individual identity and its relation to the institutions of culture. The king had come to show his image in manipulated or designed display, authored and acted, as the stage of history displaced the timeless or transcendent sphere of ritual. This emergent theatricality is something Western society has taken for granted ever since. It is the policy of modern politics to be theatrical. In *Richard II*, Shakespeare stages the process by which this theatricalization of social life became both a necessity and a new possibility. "The double medium of poetic drama," C. L. Barber wrote, "was peculiarly effective to express the struggle for omnipotence and transcendent incarnation along with its tragic and comic failure."[2]

A shattered Mirror. Before the world can become a modern theater, a mirror must be broken. Act IV, scene i: Richard and Bolingbroke meet in the climactic scene of deposition. In Ernst Kantorowicz's historical reading, the scene marks the final blow to Richard's transcendent aspirations. The king's body politic is irreparably separated from his body natural. "The fiction of the oneness of the double body breaks apart." No longer a unity of eternity and mortality, the king must face the presence of death within the crown. Richard is stripped of body politic and Godhead. "All those facets are reduced to one: to the banal face and insignificant *physis* of a miserable man, a *physis* now void of any metaphysics whatsoever. It is both less and more than death. It is the demise of Richard and the rise of a new body natural."[3]

In a play so full of expressions of grief and sorrow, the fragmented image of unity carries with it the sense of a primal loss. Richard imagines that his kingly existence will dissolve as Bolingbroke's is constituted:

> O that I were a mockery king of snow,
> Standing before the sun of Bolingbroke,
> To melt myself away in water-drops!
>
> (IV.i.260–62)

It is immediately after this wished-for loss (we might say this prayed-for loss) of identity that Richard asks for a mirror, as if the wish to dissolve leads him simultaneously to its opposite, the wish to reconfirm his power. If he is "bankrupt" (267), he still would test the power of his words: "if my word be sterling yet in England, / Let it command a mirror hither straight" (264–65). This is not a man who simply wants to lose or win; he wants to lose *and* win. Kantorowicz and others who rightly recognize the inverted ritual in the scene implicitly acknowledge that Richard's self-staging re-creates as theater a form of the omnipotent control he is also learning to relinquish. Bolingbroke grants Richard's wish for a mirror, and as so often in the play, Richard takes the occasion to center our attention on him. He makes a spectacle of himself:

> Give me that glass, and therein will I read.
> No deeper wrinkles yet? hath sorrow struck
> So many blows upon this face of mine
> And made no deeper wounds?   (IV.i.276–79)

Richard then goes on to ask rhetorically, as Marlowe's Faustus did of Helen's face, whether the image he sees reflects an inclusive self he no longer possesses:

> Was this face the face
> That everyday under his household roof
> Did keep ten thousand men? Was this the face
> That like the sun did make beholders wink?

> Is this the face which fac'd so many follies,
> That was at last out-fac'd by Bolingbroke?
>
> (IV.i.282–87)

Then, in the culmination of his punning confluence of meanings, Richard converts his sorrow and anger into an act of aggression:

> A brittle glory shineth in this face;
> As brittle as the glory is the face,
> *[Dashes the glass against the ground]*
> For there it is, crack'd in an hundred shivers.
>
> (IV.i.287–89)

Richard's "it" contains a crucial ambiguity, but before attending to it, let us note how his destruction of the mirror is as remarkable for its reversal of earlier moments in the action as it is for its overdetermined meanings in the scene. For it is precisely Richard's prevention of rage that characterizes his part in act I, scene i. "Rage must be withstood" (173), he announced to the "wrath-kindled gentlemen" (152), Bolingbroke and Mowbray. Then, in the third scene, when he intercedes immediately before the moment of violence, we see the same inhibition. Anger could not be allowed to become literal action.

Richard's destruction of the mirror raises questions about the meanings of violence in imagination and action in the play that are not fully answered by pointing out how Shakespeare is working with patterns of rite, ceremony, and pageantry. Granted, Abbot will shortly call Richard's performance "A woeful pageant" (321), and Kantorowicz identifies in Richard's actions a clear enactment of the king's *demise*, as defined in the political theology of Plowden, that demise being the divorce of the body politic from the body natural. Still, why is the violent act now literally done in a play that has until now so repetitively controlled violence, confined it to language and symbolic invitation? What does it mean that Richard actually asks for and actually breaks the mirror against the ground? And what is Bolingbroke's role in this enactment?

The act itself seems to me fascinatingly overdetermined. Indeed, it seems to be doing so many things at once that I imagine it engendering a kind of silent mixture of perplexity and recognition in the audience. The noise of shattering is followed by Richard's acknowledgment, "For there it is" (289), which is followed by Richard's address to Bolingbroke, his onstage audience: "Mark, silent King, the moral of this sport— / How soon my sorrow hath destroyed my face" (190–91).

Let us go back a few lines. Richard's play on "face" conflates the image *in* the mirror (the face he sees shows only a brittle glory, a precarious reflection of the former image of the king) with the mirror itself (as brittle as the glory reflected in the image is the face of the mirror). The mediating object is merged with the object mediated, in a confusion that reveals itself in Richard's ambiguous "it." For there *what* is? The face of the mirror? The image in the mirror? (We might pause to reflect that in the 1973 Royal Shakespeare Company's performance of the play, Richard and Bolingbroke faced one another through frame of a mirror, each seeing and reflecting the other. What was "it" then?)

The punning multiplications of meaning and the confusion are what count. Richard is refusing to look at himself, attempting to destroy the image of the reality he does recognize, and performing a magical act all at once. His moralizing interpretation does not do justice to the psychological significance of his act. He interprets it allegorically to say, in effect, "My sorrow has so quickly destroyed my glorious visage, my omnipotent self." But Bolingbroke carries the punning to a different meaning:

> The shadow of your sorrow hath destroy'd
> The shadow of your face.   (IV.i.292–93)

"The force or action of your grief (inseparable from anger) has destroyed only the image of your glorious self," is one reading. Another might be: "You have destroyed that which shadowed your face." Not the face of the man but the image of the king has been destroyed. The first reading points to the distinction between medium and mediated. The second clarifies their difference.

Now Richard himself pauses to clarify, and he recognizes the difference between the internal location of his experience and the external embodiment of his violence.

> Say that again,
> The shadow of my sorrow? Ha! Let's see—
> 'Tis very true, my grief lies all *within*,
> And these *external* manners of lament
> Are merely shadows to the unseen grief
> That swells with silence in the tortur'd soul.
>   (IV.i.293–98, italics added)

The shattered mirror, we might say, represents Richard's discovery of representation. He has begun to discover the theater, the re-creation of the shivered mirror, the shadows (actors) of absence, silence, *out there*. Richard's mirror magic, his literalization of re-flection, at once repeats and clarifies the paradox of self-representa-tion. He has enacted his *unintegrated* state—the face in the mirror shows the absence of his omnipotent self in the presence of his natural body's image—and the enactment shows the way to differ-entiate the source from the sign of that state, which is the begin-ning of *personal* integration. Richard still wishes not to be seen— he requests to be "Whither you will, so I were from your sights"— but he will be seen in a new and human light when he reappears, powerless but psychologically present as he could not be before. In bits and pieces, the king begins to *see himself* as a player—from king to I: *"Thus play I in one person many people"* (V.v.31–32, italics added). In a moment of violence that fixes our vision, the theater and the individual are born at once.

Bolingbroke and Richard Two. Is there a clue to the interdepen-dence of splitting and doubling in their names? Can it be that Bolingbroke's role in the mirror scene recapitulates an early mo-ment in the genesis of the ego in which the imagined source of rage is also the source of recognition? The Royal Shakespeare Company had these enemy twins look into one another's faces. According to D. W. Winnicott, "The precursor of the mirror is the mother's face." In the earliest phase of human development, self recognition is mediated by the states of being communicated and validated by the mother, and the subsequent sense of self remains grounded in this predifferentiated experience.[4] According to Jacques Lacan, the child's recognition of the self as a unified image is an illusion to be shattered upon conscious entry into the symbolic world of culture.[5] The two psychoanalytic positions address the inception of the "I" from opposing, yet reconcilable perspectives. Winnicott accounts for continuity of being, the sense the child develops that he is separate yet at one with the world, grounded despite conflict and loss. Lacan accounts for the dimension of unredeemable absence in human development, the phantasmic aspect of unity of being. For him, the ego is composed of "alien" images; the self is, already in its inception, imposed by the other, its language not its own.

In Shakespeare's scene of recognition, each of these perspectives has a place. Bolingbroke, as a rival, lets Richard shatter himself. He watches as Richard rages against the loss of his transcendent, timeless visage, and he will inherit the pieces that can never again be unified on the historical stage, however violent the effort. Bolingbroke, like the mother of infancy, however, helps Richard not only to lose, but also to find himself. Richard could never have spoken these lines before:

> And I thank thee, King,
> For thy great bounty, that not only giv'st
> Me cause to wail, but teaches me the way
> How to lament the cause. (IV.i.299–302)

His tone may be sarcastic, but Richard here acknowledges a shift in consciousness. The source of anger and the means of mourning are *known* to be united for the first time in his mind. (It is as if he has moved from what Melanie Klein called the paranoid-schizoid position to the depressive position. He has arrived where Hamlet begins.)

Hereafter, Richard's double divorce, from the crown and from the queen, becomes one side of the coin, the other side of which is the transposition of omnipotence into psychic theater:

> My brain I'll prove the female to my soul,
> My soul the father, and these two beget
> A generation of still-breeding thoughts,
> And these same thoughts people this little world.
> (V.v.6–9)

Richard has become a unity-in-division, perpetually uniting and dividing himself in the space of his prison, in the mortal crown of his skull. Having internalized the primal scene, he has come to represent one aspect of the Shakespearean theater, reflecting metatheatrically on its paradoxical condition. A kingdom in a nutshell. A *world*. A *little* world.

Wounds. The idea of wounding appears many times in the play. It is first introduced by Bolingbroke, who sees Richard's suggestion that he inhibit his attack as a self-wounding. He would turn his violence outward, and he justifies his high notives in terms of primitive aggression:

> Ere my tongue
> Shall wound my honour with such feeble wrong,

> Or sound so base a parle, my teeth shall tear
> The slavish motive of recanting fear,
> And spit it bleeding in his high disgrace,
> Where shame doth harbour, even in Mowbray's face.
>
> (I.i.190–95)

The logic of this counterphobic stance requires that rage find reasons in the actions of another, even if the rage is expressed in language only. The tongue, the teeth are sources of an "ancient malice" that needs to be located on some "known ground," as Richard puts the issue in his opening speeches. But the "ancient malice" can be understood as a primitive or infantile motive as well as an old theme seeking expression in the present. Like Coriolanus's son's ritualized game with his butterfly, the danger always exists that the game will collapse into sheer mouth-violence:

> I saw him run after a gilded butterfly; and when he caught
> it, he let it go again, and after it again, and over and
> over he comes, and up again; catch'd it again; or whether
> his fall enrag'd him or how 'twas, he did so set his teeth
> and tear it! O, I warrant, how he mammock'd it!
>
> (*Coriolanus*, I.iii.57–62)

Self-wounding is also Richard's fear at the moment he breaks the symmetrical confrontation between Bolingbroke and Mowbray in the third scene, but now the kingdom represents the inviolable ground:

> Draw near,
> And list what with our council we have done.
> For that our kingdom's earth should not be soil'd
> With that dear blood which it hath fostered;
> And for our eyes do hate the dire aspect
> Of *civil wounds* plough'd up with neighbours' sword.
>
> (I.iii.123–28, italics added)

In his fantasy, to act violently would be *to see* an attack on one's source, an indirect form of suicide. The dread is not only of violence, but of violence witnessed. Like Leontes, Richard stages in the mind's eye what he is loathe to recognize on the stage:

> but if one present
> Th' abhorr'd ingredient to his eye, make known
> How he hath drunk, he cracks his gorge, his sides,
> With violent hefts. I have drunk, and seen the spider.
> (*The Winter's Tale*, II.i.42–45)

After his deposition, the queen again will attempt to provoke Richard's rage in the same image:

> The lion dying thrusteth forth his paw
> And *wounds the earth*, if nothing else, with rage.
> (V.i.29–30, italics added)

To wound the earth with rage (if nothing else, an expression of power in impotence) is the unthinkable act that Richard ironically guarantees by his evasion of it. It is as if any wound is equivalent to the violation of a pristine state, a fusion of self and other writ large as the symbiosis of King and England. To disrupt this fusion would be to risk the loss of maternal containment, a ground of being. To sanction the violence between Bolingbroke and Mowbray would be "To wake our peace, which in our country's cradle / Draws the sweet infant breath of gentle sleep" (I.iii.132–33). England must remain "This nurse, this teeming womb of royal kings" (II.i.51), as Gaunt's idealization expresses the core fantasy of the timeless enclosure Richard wishes to preserve intact, untouched. He would rather yield everything than see "showers of blood / Rain'd from the wounds of slaughtered Englishmen" violate "The fresh green lap of fair King Richard's land" (III.iii.43–47).

The earth *is* wounded, however, in Richard's evocation on the coast of Wales:

> Dear earth, I do salute thee with my hand,
> Though rebels *wound* thee with their horses' hoofs.
> As a long-parted mother with her child
> Plays fondly with her tears and smiles in meeting,
> So weeping, smiling, greet I thee, my earth.
> (III.ii.6–10, italics added)

The earth wounded by others is in Richard's imagination *a child*, and he the mother who would undo the pain of separation. The roles are reversible because the maternal and infantile aspects of

existence remain precariously differentiated for Richard. He lacks a
continuous mode of defining the *relation* of self and other. He
keeps lapsing into an imaginary symbiosis with iconic versions of
himself, restaging that original unity, and then commenting on the
spectacle of his own unreal performance: "Mock not my senseless
conjuration, lords" (III.ii.23). It is as if he returns to the scene of the
child's emergence into a recognition of separateness—from the
mother, but instead of achieving stable awareness of the other as
separate from the self, he repeats the basic fault in his person. The
search for psychic constancy, therefore, takes the form of fragmen-
tary enactments, parts for wholes. "He scatters himself into a mul-
titude of images," Coleridge said, "and in conclusion endeavors to
shelter himself from that which is around him by a cloud of his
own thoughts."[6]

In the scene of the shattered mirror, the wounded ground has
become Richard's image, his face in time, which he seems to ad-
mire and pity simultaneously.

> No deeper wrinkles yet? Hath sorrow struck
> So many blows upon this face of mine
> And made no deeper *wounds*?
>
> (IV.i.277–79, italics added)

This association completes a series that connects the violence of
rebellion, the wounded earth, and the image of the king's visage, so
that the image in the mirror testifies to a vision of historical existence as a wounding, the consequence of life in time, no longer
undone by the flattering glass of kingship, or the sleep of infancy.
In fact, the mourning process has become conflated with the
trauma of recognition: sorrow strikes the blow to which it is the
response. The result of this self-referential process is a vision of
time as an agent of absence, loss of self-possession. Time circles
back to take revenge. "I wasted time, and now doth time waste
me" (V.v.49), Richard says in prison.

The question has become how to repeat the wound without con-
founding the self or the body politic, how to reconcile violence and
time. In the allegorical scene in the duke of York's garden, the
gardener says:

> We at time of year
> Do *wound* the bark, the skin of our fruit-trees,

> Lest, being over-proud in sap and blood,
> With too much riches it confound itself.
>
> > (III.iv.57–60, italics added)

The wound from without prevents the wound from within because it substitutes active violence for passive destruction, in nature's time. The "it" here is the surface—the bark, the skin—at the border between outer and inner, agent and object of action. Shakespeare's allegory images the process Freud called reality testing, the capacity to differentiate source and object of desire, to live open to pain.[7]

To repeat the wound without setting in motion self-consuming processes is, for Shakespeare, essentially an economic problem, a problem of the use and timing of action. If we understand the meanings of rage and wounding in the play as, in some fundamental psychological sense, referring to experiences of separation from imagined equivalents of a supporting, sustaining matrix with which an idealized England is associated, then the problem of history becomes one of finding or creating spaces in which that trauma can be repaired without being denied. In the figure of Richard, Shakespeare stages one alternative: denial of separation caught up in a paradoxical double movement, toward magical reenactment of symbiosis, on the one hand, and toward mournful acknowledgment of separate existence in time, on the other. Richard ends up a playwright without an audience, his shattered mirror always in the re-pair shop of himself, uniting male and female to produce an imaginary world of discontents. His separateness is isolation, helplessness before real violence. This is one way to see a condition of the theater: powerless magic, a reenactment of omnipotent creation, ever aware of its difference from the world outside. The wounded self is displayed, Christ-like, in a narcissistic repetition of an idealized state of being no longer dignified and sanctioned by a cultural fiction.

The other alternative is Bolingbroke. His separation is forced, but his rage is controlled and directed. In contrast to Richard's absorption of events into language and symbol, he acts out of awareness of the difference between thought and deed. If England is for him "My mother and my nurse that bears me yet!" (I.iii.307), he appreciates the imaginary value of that sustaining conception:

> O, who can hold a fire in his hand
> By thinking on the frosty Caucasus?
> Or cloy the hungry edge of appetite
> By bare imagination of a feast?   (I.iii.194–97)

Having accepted this distinction, Bolingbroke seems present where Richard is absent. "Gelded of his patrimony" (II.i.237), he acts strategically, metonymically as well as metaphorically. (Richard cannot negate, and, therefore, cannot be instrumental: "Learn to make a body of a limb" [III.ii.187].) He brings "fair discourse" (II.iii.6), as against the "nameless woe" (II.ii.40), that the queen laments. His language is "sweet and delectable" (II.ii.40), and it nurtures the "infant fortune" (II.iii.66) of political power. He seems already to know what Richard begins to recognize in the mirror scene. Time and timing are on his side. When York describes Bolingbroke's triumphant entry into London, he sees not only power, but mastery in time:

> Then, as I said, the Duke, great Bolingbroke,
> Mounted upon a hot and fiery steed
> Which his aspiring rider *seem'd to know*,
> With *slow but stately pace* kept on his course.
>   (V.ii.7–10, italics added)

Richard, having disrupted the organic time of custom and generational sequence, entered the paradoxical space of Shakespearean tragic experience: diminished by nourishment, fed on deprivations, like a recipient of Prospero's empty banquet, theatrically stunning, actually nothing. Bolingbroke, having reclaimed his paternal rights, having "repealed himself" (II.ii.49), seems to be restoring the economy of kingship. He moves toward Prospero's position, a theatrical guarantor of the power of the word to create action, but appears to retain personal presence in "real" time. Others find provision and freedom from separation anxiety in his promise of reparation and continuity. (As Leonard Barkan has recognized, the play itself becomes more self-consciously comedic as Bolingbroke fills the vacuum opened by Richard's evasions. In acts IV and V, we move from attempted ritual containment to comic deflections of violence.[8] "Our scene is alt'red from a serious thing, / And now chang'd to The beggar and the King"' [V.iii.77–78].)

Yet, lest we idealize Bolingbroke, let us remember that he is an exemplary political actor, always, for Shakespeare, the role of the usurper. There is policy in his psychic strategies, calculation in his capacity to offer the image of others' desires. He plays consciously to possess what Richard plays mournfully to yield. Peter Ure says that "Bolingbroke's mind and motives are in shadow,"[9] but this is the shadow of hidden or repressed desires, not Richard's present shadows of loss. For Bolingbroke shadow and silence indicate an area of *unreflected* being. He finds power in action (acting out the Oedipal theme) rather than the power that contains transcendent meaning.[10]

If Bolingbroke's theatricality, for all its manifest success, points to an absence or repression of reflective self-possession in favor of the attempt to control performance, his is the deficit that corresponds to Richard's excess. The meaning of his reality testing is ambiguous because it too involves a substitution of staging for the authority embodied in the lost integrity of the crown. Bolingbroke's theater is, therefore, the obverse of Richard's, too full of violence and lacking language. Instead of inheriting the full speech associated with ritual kingship, he finds himself bound by the issue of his own words, presented with the image of his "buried fear" (V.vi.31).

Bolingbroke's movement toward theatrical omnipotence is bound to reach a crisis. "A God on earth thou art," the duchess of York tells him. And as if the very utterance of those words, the externalization of that promised end, were the signal of a historical reality that cannot be controlled by their play, Bolingbroke answers with a dark sentence:

> But for our trusty brother-in-law and the abbot,
> With all the rest of that consorted crew,
> Destruction straight shall dog them at the heels.
> (V.iii.135–37)

But. No sooner is the promise of omnipotence spoken than it is repealed by the promise of violence. It is as if the theatricalization of experience fails from both directions to repair the wound at its source. Richard cannot integrate his version of theater into the historical scene. Bolingbroke cannot play the king without becoming guiltily caught up in repetition of the wounding process and deferred atonement. In *Richard II*, history is a play that cannot keep its form, its timing, its economy. "Can no man tell me of my unthrifty son?" (V.iii.1).

Imagine that Shakespeare looked in the mirror and saw double, two faces in one, glorious and wounded. He faced a crisis at once historical and psychological. He saw the presence of ritual meaning and iconic value in the image of human visage, but this presence was on the verge of becoming a memory. He mourned the loss of glory and raged against it. The mirror shattered and was repaired, but it would never look the same.

> For sorrow's eye, glazed with blinding tears,
> Divides one thing entire to many objects,
> Like perspectives, which, rightly gaz'd upon,
> Show nothing but confusion, ey'd awry,
> Distinguish form.   (II.ii.16–20)

The historical theater, then, enacts the paradox of a distorted clarity of representation, the same kind of paradox that defines the dilemma of the ego in psychoanalysis. Like the individual, the historical theater both is and represents a unity forever divided from itself, and its truth is inseparable from violence against time that repeats the desire for kingship. In the space opened by the loss of ritual meaning, the theater becomes diagnostic and reparative, its action always between "I play" and "I am."

State University of New York at Buffalo

NOTES

1. All quotations follow the Arden edition of *King Richard II*, ed. Peter Ure (London: Methuen and Co. Ltd., 1961).

2. "The form of Faustus' fortunes good or bad,"' *Tulane Drama Review*, 8 (1964), 92–119. Quotation is on p. 117.

3. Ernst Kantorowicz, *The King's Two Bodies: A Study in Medieval Political Theology* (Princeton: Princeton University Press, 1957), p. 40.

4. D. W. Winnicott, "Mirror-Role of Mother and Family in Child Development," in *The Predicament of the Family*, ed. Peter Lomas (New York: International Universities Press, 1967), pp. 26–33.

5. Jacques Lacan, "The Mirror Stage as Formative of the Function of the I," in *Ecrits* (New York: W. W. Norton, 1977), pp. 1–7.

6. *Coleridge on Shakespeare*, ed. R. A. Foakes (Charlottesville: The University Press of Virginia, 1971), pp. 120–21.

7. See the entry under "Reality-Testing" in J. Laplanche and J.-B. Pontalis, *The*

Language of Psycho-Analysis, trans. Donald Nicholson-Smith (New York: W. W. Norton, 1973), pp. 382–85.

8. "The Theatrical Consistency of *Richard II*," *Shakespeare Quarterly*, 29 (Winter, 1978), pp. 5–19.

9. Introduction to the Arden Shakespeare, (London: Methuen and Co. Ltd., 1961), p. lxxii.

10. In *Shakespeare's History Plays* (New York: Collier Books, 1962), E. M. W. Tillyard captured this aspect of Bolingbroke's relation to historical events: "For all his political acumen he does not know himself completely or his way about the world . . . . he has no steady policy and having once set events in motion is the servant of fortune. As such, he is not in control of events, though by his adroitness he may deal with the unpredictable as it occurs" (p. 296).